A LITTLE BOOK
—— *about* ——
A BIG STORY

Bishop Graeme Rutherford has long been committed to helping people engage with the scriptures. In this readable and user-friendly book, he walks readers through the over-arching sweep of the Bible, the Word of God written, with its focus on the living Word, the Lord Jesus Christ. Importantly, readers won't have an agenda forced on them, but will be helped to discern their part in the 'big picture' of God's story of creation and re-creation, of life and new life.

Charles Sherlock
Anglican theologian

A little book about a big story *is an important read - even if you are already familiar with the Bible as a 'big story'. In a world that tends to be suspicious of any meta-narrative, Bishop Graeme Rutherford offers fresh insights and helpful questions for what it means to live that story well today.*

Genieve Blackwell
Assistant Anglican Bishop in the Diocese of Melbourne

This is a splendid book setting its readers out on a pathway of stories, comments and interpretations, beginning with the account of the Creation as told in Genesis and ending in the coming about of the New Creation, as told in Revelation. The story lines are clearly and charmingly told, but shining through their telling is a splendid kaleidoscope of the ways in which this journey can be made sense of and brought into the centre of people's lives. The final chapter of the book brings together all these various elements and in a magical yet humble way reveals how this kind of thinking has played its part in the story of his life. This is a book which anyone – not merely students, priests and members of church congregations - can read with pleasure, engagement and insight and weave into the fabric of their own spiritual growth and personal development.

David N Aspin
Emeritus Professor, Formerly Dean of the Faculty of Education,
Head of the Graduate School, Monash University

Truth be told, this is so much more than a 'little' book. While wonderfully accessible in style, it's a book comprehensive in scope, inspiring in its breadth, and so very challenging in its convictions. What's more, it is gifted to us from the mind and heart of a man deeply shaped by the great Christian story he guides us through.

Simon Carey Holt
Collins Street Baptist Church, Melbourne

Whilst maintaining the integrity of the Biblical text, Bishop Graeme invites us to take a 'bird's eye view' of God's interaction in the world with his people from the beginning of time to the end time. This unique metanarrative he provides, invites us to draw more deeply into relationship with the One who is over all, in all and through all; the One revealed and whose purpose is fulfilled in Jesus the Christ. A delightful and much needed work.

Helen Phillips
Examining Chaplain in the Diocese of Melbourne
Vicar of St Peter's, Mornington with St Martins, Mount Martha

A LITTLE BOOK

—— *about* ——

A BIG STORY

God's grand plan
from creation
to new creation

GRAEME RUTHERFORD

a. Acorn
Press

Published by Acorn Press
An imprint of Bible Society AustraliaACN 148 058 306 | Charity licence
19 000 528
GPO Box 4161
Sydney NSW 2001
Australia
www.acornpress.net.au | www.biblesociety.org.au

ISBN 978-0-647-53362-8

First published by Morning Star Publishing in 2015,
ISBN 978-1-925-20899-3

NATIONAL
LIBRARY
OF AUSTRALIA
A catalogue record for this work is available from the National Library of Australia

Cover design and typesetting: John Healy

Dedicated in thanksgiving to God for the patient, clear-thinking scholarship and friendship of Professor C.E.B. Cranfield who died on the 27th of February, 2015, six months short of what would have been his one hundredth birthday.

He taught me that all roads in the Bible lead to Romans and all roads in Romans lead to Chapter 8 which sums up the Christian life in four great affirmations: (at the beginning) no condemnation; (at the end) no separation; (in the middle) no trepidation but eager anticipation.

CONTENTS

FOREWORD

The Christian faith is a story not a statement. It is not just a list of things to believe in. It is about God's loving purposes for the whole world and for every person. It is a story that is human and divine. It is a story that begins with God's overflowing and inventive love poured out in the creation itself. It is a story about why we get things wrong. It is a story about how God puts things right. It is a story about how the world is changed. It is a story about what happens when we die. It is the greatest story ever told. It is the big story in which all our little stories make sense. And this is a little book about this big story.

Drawing on the idea that all these stories are about friendship, Graeme Rutherford weaves into his little book all his experience as a priest and bishop, and as a teacher and preacher of the Christian faith. Every page hums with the music of a lifetime given to serving God and of living in and reflecting upon the story of God's love.

At the centre of the story is Jesus, a man not a manifesto; the one who comes from God to teach us how to be friendly, to show us how to be human. Read this compelling, accessible and illuminating book and you too will encounter Jesus. You will find your horizons elevated, your understanding of the Christian faith expanded, and your sense of God enriched. More than this, you may even find the story of your own life slowly woven into the story of God and of his loving purposes revealed in Jesus Christ, the friend of sinners.

Stephen Cottrell
Bishop of Chelmsford, England

ACKNOWLEDGMENTS

There are many people who have helped in the process of writing this book. I am especially grateful to the Rev'd Dr Charles Sherlock whose own writing and constructive criticism have helped shape the final form of a number of chapters. I also thank Emeritus Professor David Aspin along with Dr Jenneth Sasse for proof-reading the text and making many helpful comments and corrections. I am extremely honoured to have had Bishop Stephen Cottrell, the bishop of Chelmsford, to write the foreword. He has not only thought and written a great deal about the church's mission. He is a rare specimen among Anglican Bishops, especially in the Catholic tradition of Anglicanism, in being a gifted practitioner of evangelism. It was a joy to sit at his feet again at St Peter's Eastern Hill, Melbourne, during a recent parish mission. I appreciate the words of endorsement offered by Dr Charles Sherlock, Emeritus Professor David Aspin, Bishop Genieve Blackwell, Dr Simon Carey Holt and the Rev'd Helen Phillips. I thank John Healy for designing the imaginative cover and *Morning Star Publishing* for accepting this work for publication. The technical computer skills of my youngest son Jonathan have rescued me from my periodic dramas with technology. Finally, I thank my amazing wife Caroline who, as ever, has been right behind me every step of the way. Without her encouragement and companionship on the journey, I couldn't keep on doing what I know I should. She has patiently coped with my reclusive existence and failed retirement promise to play my part in the kitchen. I will be the 'big chief chef' from now on. Promise!

INTRODUCTION

In today's religiously plural climate it has become fashionable to speak of different 'Faith Groups'. It's a way of describing religious groupings who have a 'faith' that shapes the way they view the world and motivates what they do – it includes Jews, Christians, Muslims, Hindus, Buddhists, Sikhs and many others. But this terminology raises the question - what counts as a Faith Group? In questioning this way of speaking, Graham Tomlin is right to ask:

> What are all the others? What about secular humanists, atheists, socialists, communists? What are they? They also are united by certain core beliefs about human life and its purpose. They also are motivated for action in society, and attempt to build a better one by those beliefs. So what are they, if they are not 'Faith Groups'? 'Reason Groups' or, perhaps, 'Truth Groups'?[1]

The problem for Tomlin, in speaking about 'Faith Groups', is that it boxes religions into a special category, as if religious people alone have a 'faith' (something that we assume to be a lesser form of knowledge than 'proof' or 'reason') and all the others are based on something other than faith.

But Christians are not alone in basing their lifestyle on faith. Atheists, socialists and secular humanists all have faith. All of them adopt as certain the available evidence such as that we appear to be alone in the universe without any superior being (atheism). In saying this, Tomlin has no wish to belittle these positions or to argue that they are false. His intention is, 'simply to call them what they are: positions adopted through faith'. Theists cannot 'prove' God's existence any more than Atheists can 'disprove' it. We do not need to cower before others because of our own felt need to exercise faith. That we can mull over and weigh up whether to make the surrender of faith highlights that faith in God can be compatible with the exercise of our reason, rather

---

1 Graham Tomlin, *'Living out of Stories'*, grahamtomlin.blogspot.com/

than the denial of it. As the Roman Catholic theologian Richard Lennan says, 'Although such discernment will not eliminate the risk of faith, it does ensure that faith is less of a leap into the dark than a leap into what we hope will be the light'.[2]

This leap of faith is crucial because it establishes a new relationship that is of a different order than that which led up to it. It becomes a person-to-person relationship, a mutual presence, involving inner commitment and acceptance, no longer totally reliant on the balance of positive and negative factors. Moreover, if this leap of faith cannot be confined to religious belief and practice, the designation 'Faith Groups' is of little use in distinguishing those who believe in a world without God (atheists) and those who believe in a world with God (theists). How then should we speak?

Living out of different stories

Graham Tomlin concludes that thinking in terms of different 'narratives' or 'stories' is a better way to speak because it recognises that these 'stories' shape the identities and assumptions of those in any group, whether or not it is religious. Christians are not people who somehow adopt a 'faith' while secular humanists don't. Tomlin rightly says: 'Everyone lives by a story. Everyone has a faith. So let's stop pretending that only some do'. The fact that a person does not believe in God does not mean that such a person ceases to believe at all. Faith is just a part of being human. I am personally persuaded of the truth of the Bible not because I have logically coercive proof but because it provides a *'big picture'* of reality that offers the best *'empirical fit'* to what I observe within me and around me. This means that, against the all-pervasive influence of science, which has its own tested principles of verification appropriate to its own field, those of us who have faith in God usually have some unlearning to do before we can begin to *'trust in trust'* and *'stand firm in faith'*.

---

2 Richard Lennan, *Risking the Church*, (Oxford University Press, 2004), 65

Ordinary laid-back Aussies rarely give any serious consideration to the deep things that shape their life. Commenting on the way in which sport functions as a kind of religion for many Australian men and women, Roy Williams says:

> The whole point is to invest significance in something that really does not matter a fig – in this world, let alone the next. I write as a lifelong lover of sport, as both player and spectator. Take the devoted football team (any code, but imagine AFL). He (*sic*) arranges his life around the team's schedule, in the same way as a medieval Christian used to arrange his life around the days of the Church's year. He invests much of his physical and emotional energy in the cause. His rituals are religious in character: regular fellowship with co-enthusiasts, endless pontification about points of detail, communal singing or chanting, worship of heroes and denunciation of villains. And, always, an eye on the ultimate prize (the premiership, or whatever) is, at its core, meaningless – especially if it can only be achieved vicariously, through the efforts of others.[3]

Roy Williams has put his finger on one of the big problems that the Christian church faces today. In our casual, easy-going culture there is often a 'suspension of a serious worldview'. It is not simply that the Bible's metanarrative is not believed but that it is virtually unknown. Not only those outside the church but many inside the church have little or no understanding of the Scripture's overarching storyline. My parents seldom went to church but they sent me to Sunday-School where I heard some of the Biblical stories such as 'David and Goliath', 'Jonah in the whale's belly' and 'Daniel in the Lion's den'. Even so, I had no idea how these different stories hang together to form a coherent narrative.

A worldview with explanatory power

It has been said that what is needed is a 'clothesline' on which to hang the various bits and pieces of the Bible's story that people may have heard or read about. My aim in writing this book is to provide such a clothesline.

3 Roy Williams, *Post God Nation?* (HarperCollins Australia, 2015) 278

Walter Brueggemann has defined Christian conversion as 'the re-storying of one's life in the stories of the Bible'. In order to do this we need to know and appreciate the main twists and turns in this panoramic journey as it picks its way across the complex, broken, mountainous landscape of history. In ordinary political terms Israel was a tiny nation constantly ruled and oppressed by neighbouring super-power nations, yet the Old Testament tells its story as though Israel was the most important nation on earth. All human history, according to the Old Testament, found its focus in the unfolding story of Israel. In the chapters that follow, we will consider the framework of the big story of both the Old and the New Testaments as it stretches through six distinct dramatic acts: Creation; De-creation, Israel; Messiah; Church; New Creation. It has been rightly said that stories don't come much bigger than this.

Presuppositions

Everyone has presuppositions. The 'pre' part of this word means 'before' and the 'suppositions' are what is supposed, what is assumed and taken for granted to be true. Presuppositions are assumptions that we make ahead of time. In writing this book I unapologetically lay my three basic presuppositions on the table. First, *God exists*. The Bible nowhere attempts to prove this but assumes it to be true from the beginning. Second, *God acts*. He acts to rescue his people and to complete his creation. In the Old Testament, God rescues the people of Israel from slavery in Egypt and from exile in Babylon. These events point to the New Testament account of God's redeeming activity in rescuing sinners from the slavery of sin and death through the death and resurrection of Jesus. Although historians, acting as historians, may be able to throw some light on the veracity of the historical reporting, they cannot as I shall argue, prove that God was active in these 'uniquely, unique' events. The Bible comprises of what both Israel and the early Christian community wanted people to remember. Both Testaments are the embodiment of a 'collective memory'. The significance of memory is underlined by both Jesus and Paul: 'Do this in remembrance of me'

(Luke 22.19; 1 Corinthians 11.24). This notion of memory presupposes the selective nature of their relationship with the past.[4] Third, *God speaks*. Unlike the heathen idols, 'who have mouths but do not speak', God is not dumb, locked up in Godself (Psalm 115.5). Nor does God play a game of hide and seek from us, as some of the 'apophatic' mystical writers claim. The author of 'The Cloud of Unknowing' is typical of this so-called 'negative way', stressing that God is ineffable and incomprehensible. However, despite the inadequacy of human language, God delights to make Godself known. Outgoingness, self-expression and self-communication are of God's essence.

These three assumptions lie behind my belief that the books that make up the Bible, though clearly deriving from human authors employing a variety of literary genres nevertheless had their origins in God like no other body of literature. Nowhere does Scripture explain how divine inspiration and human authorship connect. The Biblical authors are not interested in such metaphysical matters. They simply assert that God is made known in special revelation now crystallized as Holy Scripture (Hebrews 1.1,2 and 2 Timothy 3.16,17). The Scriptures have a mysterious, double authorship, in which divine providence acts simultaneously with human authors and the resulting self-disclosure of God that they give us, is no misrepresentation. God is no bungler. God is a reliable communicator. God is telling the 'big story' as its author and main actor. Indeed, it has been suggested that the Bible is 'God's authorised biography. Perhaps even an autobiography with ghost writers'.[5] The whole story hangs together as an account of the promises of God and of how God has kept those promises in the realm of human history. The epicentre of the story concerns God's activity in the death and resurrection of Jesus for the flourishing of all people of all ages. Without a reliable record of this climactic event, God would have defeated God's own purpose. Such a high view of Scripture does not commit a person to a naïve, fundamentalist hermeneutic as in the bumper-

---

4 For a fascinating study of the nature and importance of memory in the Bible see John Goldingay, *Do we need the New Testament?* (IVP Academic, 2015)
5 John H. Walton & Kim E. Walton, *The Bible Story Handbook*, (Crossway, 2010), 14

sticker slogan: 'God said it; I believe it; that settles it'. Inspiration is not the same as dictation. As John Stackhouse has put it, 'We do not reside on an epistemological Gibraltar. We must interpret the Bible'[6]. A robust view of revelation demands a conscientious commitment to the task of careful exegesis. Sadly, there is often a scandalous dichotomy between how the Scripture is regarded and how it is treated.

To view the Bible's inspiration and authority as outlined above has led some people to regard Christians as: 'the People of the Book'. But John Dominic Crossan has suggested that a better shorthand expression for Christians might be: 'the People *with* the Book' and 'even more importantly, ... "the People of the Person."'[7] If this is correct, and I think it is, the Bible should be approached as divine discourse through which we allow the Spirit to actualize the Word of God in our lives, showing us how we are to relate to God, each other and the whole world around us. It is not a book concerned solely for passing on information about God. Rather, it is an invitation to a relationship with God. The interest of those who wrote down the texts which make up the Bible is primarily existential. For them, knowing God is not simply a matter of intellectual description, whether of empirical science or historical fact. Nor is it primarily a matter of regulation and rules, telling us what we 'ought to do' or 'should do'. Such mantras are backward looking and destructive. Fr Patrick O'Sullivan SJ has warned that such a misunderstanding of the Bible's purpose leads to a 'hardening of the oughteries'! Many of the commands recorded in the Bible do not oblige us to obey them. They must be understood within their context in the Biblical story. It is

---

6 John Stackhouse, *Need to Know – Vocation as the heart of Christian Epistemology,* (Oxford University Press, 20).

7 John Dominic Crossan, *How To Read The Bible & Still Be A Christian,* (HarperOne, 2015), 35. Although I agree with Crossan's emphasis on the necessity for a 'relationship with Christ' as being fundamental to the purpose of the Bible, it must be a relationship with the *Christ of the Bible*, not simply the *Christ of history* as authenticated by the findings of the Jesus Seminar scholars. The Scriptures are the God-given means through which we know who Jesus is. If we apply the editorial pen to the Bible in the way that Crossan does in his book, we are in danger of inventing a Jesus different from the Jesus revealed in the Bible. We are also in danger of usurping the authority that properly belongs to God, the God who has invested authority in the Jesus of the written text of the Scriptures.

likely that some of the instructions in the Old Testament were intended for the nation of Israel only. The Biblical story is primary and it defines the authority of commands contextually. What is clear is that in the Bible, morality always arises out of a prior knowledge of God and God's grace. God's commands express the authority of grace.

Knowing God is essentially a matter of relationship, *'knowledge by acquaintance'*. In this regard, although human logic may be rationally adequate, it will always be existentially deficient. Moreover, *'knowledge by acquaintance'* must not be regarded as a nodding acquaintance. Just as we can only get to know other people intimately as we share stories from our past, present and future hopes, so likewise we are to read and inhabit the Bible, which is God's story, in order to get intimately involved with the living God. We are 'creatures-for-communion'. As C. S. Lewis once put it, 'in Christianity we are not faced with an argument which demands our assent but with a Person who demands our confidence'. James makes it clear that there is a world of difference between rational acceptance and personal transformation when he writes: 'You believe that God is one; you do well. Even the demons believe – and shudder (James 2.19). The demons have all the right ideas but it would be eccentric to call them 'believers'.

A former bishop of Oxford, John Pritchard, has suggested a helpful way of teaching children that relationship is a key to understanding the six distinctive acts of the Biblical drama listed above. He sums it up neatly:

Making friends – the creation
Friends fall out – the Fall
Friends keep trying – the story of Israel
The best, best friend – Jesus
Friends together – the church
Friends forever – the new creation[8]

More often than not, as I reflect on some part of the jigsaw of God's story in the Bible, God shows me the need to reconfigure my life in conformity to Christ in some way. I become aware that if my relationship with

---

8 John Pritchard, *Living faithfully: Following Christ in everyday life*, (SPCK, 2013), 118

God is to grow I have to get serious. It is the same in any relationship. There comes a moment of commitment. Up until that point, we keep our options open, looking in from the outside. Commitment is about looking from the inside out. Anna in the book, *Mister God, This is Anna,* tries hard to explain to her adult male friend Fynn that God understands us from the inside:

'Fynn, Mister God doesn't love us'. She hesitated. 'He doesn't really, you know, only people can love. I love Bossy the cat but Bossy don't love me. I love the pollywogs, but they don't love me. I love you, Fynn, and you love me, don't you'? I tightened my arm about her. 'You love me because you are people. I love Mister God truly, but he don't love me'. It sounded like a death knell. 'Damn and blast', I thought. 'Why does this have to happen to people? Now she's lost everything'. But I was wrong. She has got both feet planted firmly on the next stepping stone. 'No', she went on, 'no, he don't love me, not like you do, it's different, its millions of times bigger'. ... 'You see, Fynn, people can only love outside, and can only kiss outside, but Mister God can love you right inside, and Mister God can kiss you right inside, so it's different. Mister God ain't like us; we are a little bit like Mister God, but not much yet'.[9]

My hope and prayer in writing this *'Little Book about a Big Story'* is that readers will catch something of Anna's 'millions time bigger' perception of the Bible's rich relational tones. We constantly under estimate the scale of God's love. But the Bible does not confine its teaching about relating to God to the interior life of prayer. Too often, 'religious talk is about religious talk'.[10] Life becomes a footnote. But knowledge of God in the Bible is never a footnote. In the chapters ahead, we shall see how the Bible's story offers a magnificent, rich and deep account of God, the world and our place in it. It speaks into concrete situations such as how we are to relate in: our workplaces, our marriages, our friendships, our times of suffering and facing death. In addition, it challenges us to be

9 Fynn, *Mister God, This is Anna,* (Collins, 1974), 41
10 Michael Bernard Kelly, *Seduced by Grace: Contemporary spirituality, Gay experience and Christian faith.* (Melbourne: Clouds of Magellan Publishing,) 2007

involved with the poor; the refugees and other marginalized people as well as the crisis facing the global environment.

Like any relationship, a relationship with God does not flourish on nice thoughts. The acid test for any theology is not how intellectually erudite it is but whether it brings us into the realm of encounter with the God into whom we enquire with our minds. Unless it does that, our theological study will be arid, divisive and dull. The early Greek theologians always envisaged that theology must be done by invoking (*'epiclesis'*) the help of the Spirit who alone can draw us into the intimate life and love of the Triune God. Such a theology gets done within that experience, not outside of it. That is why Paul prayed that the believers in Ephesus would have the power to understand just how wide, how long, how high and how deep God's love is (Ephesians 3.18). It is a matter of the heart as well as the mind.

Yet an even more important fact is that God's gracious, unfailing love always precedes our response to it. The great Anglo-Catholic historian, Owen Chadwick makes this point well when he writes:

> Underneath the worship of God lies silence, a wordless praise, an eyeless vision. When a mind gets faith, it does not get it as it gets a knowledge of England's history, or as it gets a knowledge of sparking plugs. For *gets* is the wrong word. The word which rings true is not *gets* but *receives*. If you have faith at all, you feel as though you have received it. You hardly asked for it. You may not have wanted it. It came.[11]

Accepting a gospel of grace is a major challenge to a culture that values everything in terms of financial exchange. Faith cannot be reduced to a transaction that says, 'If I do what is right, God will keep me safe from harm'. It is not a matter of 'spiritual accountancy'. The notion of earning grace is a contradiction in terms. The superabundance of grace is *'grace gone ga-ga'*.[12] It is totally illogical. I am a Christian by grace alone. In

---

11 Owen Chadwick, *The Spirit of the Oxford Movement*, (Cambridge University Press, 1990), 307

12 See www.faith-theology.com/ Monday, 14th September, 2015, *Can we stand it? A*

the final analysis, it is not the case that 'Graeme found grace'. It's the reverse. 'Grace found Graeme'. In the words of an anonymous poet:

Let me no more my comfort draw
From my frail hold of Thee.
In this alone rejoice with awe –
Thy mighty grasp of me.[13]

Questions for reflection

1. Christian conversion is 're-storying of our life in the story of the Bible.' How would you describe your current story? Is it busy and hectic; full of mid-life blues; excited about the future or anxious about the future? Share something of your own story with others in the group and/or write about it in a journal.

2. John Goldingay writes: 'A narrative is an account of a sequence of events. The link between narrative and worldview is that narrative is a natural carrier of a worldview'.[14] The 'big story' we are considering in this 'little book' expresses a total world view. It embraces a Beginning, an End and events on the narrative line in between ('middle narrative'). How has the Biblical narrative changed the way you think and behave?

3. The author implies that integrity consists *not* in having no presuppositions. Rather, integrity consists in being aware of what one's presuppositions are. What are the presuppositions on which your worldview is based?

sermon for Racial Justice Sunday, posted by Kim Fabricius
13 Denis Duncan, *Toward the light: Prayers through depression to healing*, (SPCK, 2009), 8
14 John Goldingay, *Do we need the New Testament?* (IVP Academic, 2015), 70

1. The Story of Creation

Some careers involve uprooting and moving house on a fairly frequent basis. As a member of the clergy I have lived in seven different houses. The very sight of a Removalist Van backing into the yard and the thought of packing and un-packing and subsequent setting up a home can throw me into apoplexy. Fortunately, I am married to a wonderful home-maker. And that, according to a leading Old Testament scholar, John Walton, was the challenge that confronted the Creator God in the opening majestic chapter of the Bible – Genesis chapter 1. That chapter, Walton claims, is a 'home-story' not a 'house-story'. He explains the difference as follows:

> In investigating a new location in which to live, some members of the family might examine the physical structure of the house. Roof, foundation, electricity, plumbing, furnace and general condition are all of immense importance. At the same time, others in the family may be assessing how the house will serve as a home. Domestic traffic patterns and open design are only the beginning. Which room will be used in which way? Where will the furniture fit? The kids are most likely to run upstairs to figure out which rooms will be theirs. In this way, some are considering the house; the others are considering the home.[1]

According to John Walton, it would not have been difficult for a reader from anywhere in the Ancient Near East to draw the conclusion that Genesis chapter 1 was a 'home story' rather than a 'house story'. God's purpose in the six creation days was to order the creation in such a way that it became a home for people and a home for God-self. The ancient author's account of creation in Genesis chapter 1 has little if anything to do with material origins - 'building a house'. It is about ordering the cosmos so that it becomes a 'home' in which God can dwell. From his research into Ancient Near Eastern culture, Walton supports this claim with two crucial insights – (a.) ordering of the chaos and (b.) occupying sacred space.

---

1 John H. Walton, *The Lost World of Adam and Eve*, (IVP, 2015), 44,45

Ordering chaos

The Hebrew verb '*bara*' translated in most English Bibles as 'create' does not describe the creation of the material world out of nothing – as though it came into being by a special divine decree. There are many passages in both the Old and New Testaments that do speak of creation in this way, most notably, the prologue of John's Gospel:

> All things came into being through him (the Logos/Word), and without him not one thing came into being (John 1:3).

Paul says the same thing in Colossians:

> All things have been created through him and for him (Colossians 1.16).

But this is not how Genesis 1 speaks about creation. Rather '*bara*' has to do with shaping and ordering 'the disorder of the yet-to-be-formed places', filling them and assigning function to the various functionaries as the chapter unfolds. This interpretation is supported by Genesis 1:1,2 which implies that matter already exists:

> In the beginning when God created the heavens and the earth, the earth was void and darkness covered the face of the deep, while a wind from God swept over the face of the waters.

What God does in the six creation days is to bring order and structure to this formless mass; fill it with animals, birds and fish and then ascribe a distinct role and responsibility to humanity within the creation. In the first half of the week of creation, (days 1-3) the cosmos is ordered by the separation of light from darkness so that day and night alternate as the world's metronome, evening and morning, evening and morning, evening and morning and so on up to the present. This is followed by a Sky-making day when God sets a great rock-solid dome in the sky - 'the firmament', to separate water from water, above and below. The waters below the firmament are further separated into land and sea. When it rained, the water was believed to come through gaps or windows in the dome.

In the second half of the week (days 4-6) the ordered spaces of sky, land and sea are filled. *Sky space* is filled with sun, moon, stars and birds (and no doubt, other planets). *Sea space* is populated with vast range of fish and sea monsters. Then on day six, *Earth space* is filled with animals. From day three onwards God gives reproductive potential to the world by releasing creation to create: 'Then God said, "Let the earth put forth vegetation: plants yielding seed, and fruit trees of every kind on earth that bear fruit with seed in it" (Genesis 1.11). Finally, on the sixth day, humans are created as a reflection of God within creation, not in the likeness of anything on earth. Men and women, uniquely among created beings, are to exercise a delegated divine authority by enabling the creation to be an ordered and fruitful place.

This first creation story (Genesis 1.1 – 2.4a) is told with Hebrew poetic rhythm and repetition. In fact there is so much rhythm in this chapter that someone has suggested: 'you can only conclude that God must be black? There's too much rhythm here for God to be white'. What is clear is that the focus of Genesis 1 with all its poetic rhythm is not about the making of stuff but about the ordering of chaos and ascribing function to the various parts, including human beings, over the six creation days.

The second creation story in Genesis 2.4-25 is a sequel to the cosmic account in chapter one. It zooms down into a garden or rather, a large national park and commences with the creation of Adam from pre-existent created matter, 'the dust of the ground' (2.7). The two hands depicted at the top of the cover of this book represent Michelangelo's famous fresco in the Sistine Chapel.[2] A preacher explains the meaning of the painting in this way:

> God's finger is stretched out towards Adam. Within the next second, life and power will be transmitted from finger-tip to finger-tip. We wait for the spark to leap across the gap. We know that this means the creation of Adam, the moment when the life of the spirit enters his body. After this contact he will no longer be a clod of earth, or dust, or animal but a living soul.[3]

2 The cover was designed by John Healy.
3 David Day, *Pearl Beyond Price: The Attractive Jesus*, (Zondervan, 2001), 77

Later Eve is created from already-formed bodily matter – out of the rib of Adam. Adam and Eve are here presented as archetypes rather than individuals, expressing something that is true of all humans. Once again, we must notice, as in Genesis 1, that the ancient authors are not writing about material origins. They had no knowledge of chemistry. Alister McGrath allows his scientific background to mislead him into claiming that, because Adam was formed 'from the dust,' humans are a 'walking collection of chemicals'. He goes on to make a quick calculation that each human 'could be reduced to enough water to have a shower and enough fat to make half a dozen bars of soap'.[4] Given his expertise, I would not presume to dispute the accuracy of his chemical analysis. But in the light of Walton's careful research in to Ancient Near Eastern cosmologies, I am not persuaded that the chemical composition of humanity is what the ancient author of Genesis had in mind.

Walton employs a modern analogy to help us to grasp the distinction between functional and material origins. He asks his readers to consider the making of a computer and goes on to point out that there are many stages in the process:

> At the most basic level the casing and the electronics have to be manufactured, the keyboard and other peripherals designed and so forth. This is the basic production and manufacturing process – what we might call the material phase of production. But another aspect involves writing the programs. Even after those programs are written, if the software has not been installed on the computer, its "existence" is meaningless – it cannot function. So there is a separate process of installing the software that makes the computer theoretically functional. But what if there is no power source (electric or battery)? This is another obstacle to the computer's existence. Adding a power source, we might now claim that its existence is finally and completely achieved. But what if no one sits on the keyboard or knows how to use or even desires to use it? It remains non-functional, and, for all intents and purposes, as if it did not exist. We can see that different observers might be inclined to attribute

4 Alister McGrath, *The Spirit of Grace*, (SPCK, 2015), 24

"existence" to the computer at different stages in the process. ...
In the ancient world, what was most crucial and significant to their
understanding of existence was the way that the parts of the cosmos
functioned, not their material status.[5]

Genesis 1 is not about the making of material 'stuff'. It is about ordering
the chaos and assigning function.

Sacred Space

A second key insight from Ancient Near Eastern culture that shapes
Walton's exegesis of Genesis 1 concerns God's rest on the seventh day.
He argues that God's rest does not refer to taking time-off for a nap.
The psalmist says that the God who keeps Israel will 'neither slumber
nor sleep' (Psalm 121.4). Taking rest has to do with God/gods coming
to occupy the newly ordered cosmos as a newly created cosmic temple.
The seven day structure of Genesis 1 corresponds to a traditional
seven-day temple inauguration. The number seven is common in all
the dedication ceremonies of pagan temples to the gods. It occurs in the
Bible with Solomon's dedication ritual of the new temple in 1 Kings
8:65. After a seven day period, it was believed that God would come
and take up residence in the temple as the throne room of creation.
Solomon finishes this great service of dedication and down comes the
glory of God like a thick, choking cloud (1 Kings 8.10,11). The priests
were unable to stay there because the glory was so intense they couldn't
breathe! Their running out of the temple was not because of hysteria. It
was an experience of raw God. Raw God is terrifyingly powerful. It is
this power that sustains creation. Were God to withdraw his power, even
for a moment, the *cosmos* would fall back into *chaos*. Sinful humans
cannot bear too much of the glory of God's presence. This powerful
Old Testament image of the priests leaving the newly dedicated temple
because they couldn't bear God's glory is taken up in the last verse of
the familiar hymn, *Immortal, invisible, God only wise*:

5 John H. Walton, *The Lost World Of Genesis One*, (IVP, 2009), 24,25

Great Father of glory, pure Father of light,
Thine angels adore thee, all veiling their sight;
All laud we would render: O help us to see
'Tis only the splendour of light hideth thee.

The Sabbath represents God's taking his place at the command centre, the 'sacred space' of creation. Even if our eyes are veiled and unable to pick up the clues from his open-handed generosity and crazy abundance, God is nevertheless, in the control room of creation, maintaining order and exercising sovereignty. God's sovereignty and interaction with his world, as John Pritchard has said, is possibly much better seen 'as undertaken from the inside rather than the outside - God 'under-rules' rather than 'over-rules'.[6] Scientists have drawn attention to the fine-tuning of our universe in speaking of the 'anthropic principle'. This refers to certain cosmological constants, which if varied even slightly, would have significant implications for human existence. These constants turn out to be fine-tuned, life-friendly values. Such research does not provide knock-down proof for a Creator God but it is highly suggestive. At the very least, we can say that there is a correspondence between the 'anthropic principle' and the Genesis 1 understanding of creation as the control room of a Creator who turns the dials on the 'cosmic control panel'. God is *other* than creation and yet, intimately and dynamically related to creation.

A warning

In the light of Walton's research, we may maintain that both the 'six-day creationists' and 'theistic evolutionists' make a category mistake in reading the chapter by the concepts and criteria of true or false science. The seven days had nothing to do with the time in which the material world was created – whether by the Word of God in six, twenty-four hour days, as in the case of the 'six day creationists' or in 13.5 billion years, as in the case of 'theistic evolutionists'. There is no need to extend the six days of creation into geological epochs. The scientific worldview is the water that we Westerners swim in but this story doesn't oblige us to

---

6 John Pritchard, *Living Faithfully*, (SPCK, 2013), 28

wonder how dinosaurs fit into the picture. Walton argues that Genesis chapter 1 has nothing to do with science at all. Unconsciously, we bring our scientific worldview to the interpretation of this chapter. We too easily overlook the fact that this narrative was written by an author who did not possess our scientific worldview, to an audience who did not possess our scientific worldview.

To understand the text the way it was meant to be understood, we need to think like an ancient Hebrew, not a modern Westerner. God's revelation in the Bible was not given in a hermetically sealed bubble, via dictation. God chose to use human authors who wrote out of their own cultural context and understanding. According to Walton, if we are to understand these opening stories of the Bible correctly, we must read them in the context of their own time and culture, just as a missionary to a foreign country has to learn the language and culture of the country in which they are called to communicate the gospel message. No missionary would think of saying to those to whom they have been sent, 'if you are going to understand my message, you have got to learn my language'. Rather, every missionary takes the time and trouble to learn the language and customs of the people to whom they are called to minister. Likewise the reader of the Bible cannot avoid the hard work of interpretation.

As we have seen, Walton argues that in Genesis chapter 1, the seven days reflect the Ancient Near Eastern liturgical practice of a seven day inauguration ceremony of a new temple. In the ancient cultures of Egypt and Mesopotamia, it was believed that during this religious ceremony the gods took up residence and began to reign from within the newly blessed 'sacred space'. Likewise, when God is said to have rested on the seventh day in Genesis 2.1-3, God was understood to be at the hub of control, the executive office of creation. In communicating these things, God bound God-self to a culture – not Greek culture; not medieval culture; but Ancient Near Eastern culture. God's rest on the seventh day would communicate to the ancient readers that God is present in creation; God is passionately committed to its good and God desires relationship with humans.

It has been said that, in the medieval period when great tracts of the world were still unknown and still unexplored, maps were drawn and on the blank unknown spaces cartographers wrote: 'Here be burning fiery sands'. But the Sabbath rest was intended to assure us that we can write across every bit of the map: 'Here is God'. The whole creation is 'sacred space'. None of it is beyond revealing God's glory. In fact, as we shall see, the incarnation makes it clear that God delights in being revealed in places like a humble, dirty stable. More particularly, God is the earth's landlord and we are God's tenants. God holds us accountable for our treatment of divine property.

Human accountability arises from our being in the 'the image of God'. That phrase is widely regarded today as having more to do with our role in creation than our intellectual, moral or spiritual abilities. Out of all the species of animals on earth, humanity is chosen to have a unique vocation. This human vocation, seen in the light of the Genesis story, is a challenge to us to face the urgent contemporary problem of climate change. No other generation has had to face up to what the vast mass of scientists agree is human-induced climate change, and the knowledge that their action or inaction will determine the future of life on the planet. To be unconcerned about this prospect is to be either desperately ignorant or irresponsibly callous. Speaking of this human vocation, Graham Tomlin says:

> This is a vision of the world that gives a special, particular role to humanity, yet it is not at all anthropocentric. On this account, the world is not made for humanity; rather it is the other way round: humanity is made to care for and nurture the rest of creation.[7]

Richard Bauckham has cautioned against giving human beings too prominent a role in protecting and nurturing creation, preferring to

---

7 Graham Tomlin, *The Widening Circle: Priesthood as God's way of blessing the world,* (SPCK, 2014), 78

speak of humans as part of 'the community of creation'.[8] Whilst Tomlin acknowledges the truth about the interdependence of the ecological systems he persists in arguing that the Genesis stories give a unique role to humankind as reflecting the divine creativity in many ways. He says:

> The nurturing and enhancement of life on earth does require human activity. Grain does not turn into bread on its own. Chemicals do not turn into medicine spontaneously. Marble does not miraculously form itself into Michelangelo's 'David' by chance. Technology, medicine and art all enhance and protect life and Creation itself, and all are part of the human priestly calling to mediate God's love to Creation, bringing the joy which was its true purpose.[9]

According to Tomlin, the Genesis creation accounts present human beings as having a priestly function in relation to creation. He points out that priests were part of the furniture of first century religion, both Jewish and pagan and it should not surprise us that in the Bible, there is a widening circle of blessing through a priestly ministry spreading out from Jesus Christ, the true High Priest who stands between God and humanity. Jesus, our great High Priest, unites divinity and humanity by being both divine and human (Hebrews 2.17). In his priestly identity and priestly offering, Jesus is unique. There is no other priest. Nowhere in the New Testament is the word 'priest' applied to church leaders (regardless of what Roman Catholics, Orthodox Christians and Anglicans say!) However, the New Testament does suggest that Christ's priesthood was shared with the church. In the Old Testament, the nation of Israel is spoken of as a priestly nation and in the New Testament this same language is applied to the church:

> But you are a chosen race, a royal priesthood, a holy nation, God's own people, in order that you may proclaim the mighty acts of him who called you out of darkness into his marvellous light (1 Peter 2.9).

---

8 Richard Bauckham, *Living with other creatures: Green exegesis and theology*, (Paternoster, 2012), 151f
9 Tomlin, op.cit., 89

As a 'royal priesthood' the church has a part to play in looking after God's world (that's the royal bit) and to be a mirror reflecting the praises, thanksgiving and intercessions of all creation back to the Creator (that's the priestly bit). Rightly understood, this is a ministry that ought to help us to let go of the idea that creation is just there for the use of humanity. The widening circle of blessing stretches from radical *dependence* on Christ, the unique priest, into radical *interdependence* on each other within the church. At this point in his spiralling priestly circle of blessing, Tomlin makes an important qualification. He says:

> It is not primarily the Church's calling to care for Creation: that is a human calling. As Church we do our bit, but we rejoice every time technology produces useful things, flood defences are raised and laws are passed to protect green fields or rain forests.[10]

This qualifying truth makes the church's role a little bit more manageable.

The widest circle of priestly blessing is the responsibility of the whole of humanity. It is not a responsibility that can be left to one particular side of the political spectrum. It must be the concern of all political parties. Far too often in public debate, the two big 'e' words, *ecology* and *economy*, have been used as though they represented opposing concerns. Some politicians are prepared to tackle environmental issues so long as they don't interfere with economic development and the liberty to create wealth in whatever way is possible. Others are glad to address environmental issues so long as the challenge of economic injustice within the nation is first resolved. In recognizing that 'the economy is a wholly-owned subsidiary of the environment' Pope Francis has gone where few public figures fear to go in challenging the selfish nature of capitalism and calling for a new economic order. He has made it clear that as we move into the future it is not a matter of making a choice between looking after human beings and looking after the planet. The health of the world around us and our own long-term health are not two things, but one. The *economy* and *ecology* cannot be separated because the knock-on effect from economic development is a positive depletion

---

10 Tomlin, op.cit., 157, 158

of real wealth in terms of natural capital. There is a point beyond which the natural order cannot continue to operate 'normally'.

The ecological agenda is always vulnerable to the pressure of other more apparently 'immediate' issues and therefore cannot be left to electoral politics alone. It is up to us consumers and voters to do the little bit we can for the sake of the 'sacred space' we have been invited to nurture and protect. Taking steps of courage and generosity for the sake of the environment will undoubtedly make us a little less comfortable. The implication of Pope Francis's clarion call in the encyclical letter[11] is that it is high time the Christian churches were able to say loudly and clearly and unanimously: *So what?*

Creation care is not an obligation resting on experts and enthusiasts alone. In addition to international and national agreements a steady background of awareness and small-scale committed action has been entrusted to all humankind without exception. As the well-known maxim puts it, we are to 'think globally but act locally'. There is a sense in which the kingdom of God is a political image. As such, it is an image of God's relationship to the whole creation, not just his own people. The presence of God's kingdom is for the most part occasional and small-scale but it makes a considerable difference to the everyday. As an anonymous sage says:

I'm only one,
But I am one.
I can't do everything,
But I can do something.
What I can do,
I ought to do.
And what I ought to do,
By the grace of God
I will do.

---

11 *Laudato Si' (God be praised): On care for our common home.*

Questions for reflection

1. How do you think that reading Genesis 1 in the light of Ancient Near Eastern thinking can help build bridges between 'creationists' and those who adopt modern scientific theories of evolution?

2. The Ancient Near Eastern creation stories employ a seven day inauguration ceremony to represent the god's taking up residence in a temple. In what ways, if any, do you find this insight helpful in interpreting Genesis 1.

3. In the Christian Orthodox tradition, icons are intended to lead people through the thin veil that separates heaven and earth, into the very presence of God. Bishop Tom Wright has said that, 'Christian artists have a unique vocation of enabling people to see what they can't otherwise see, to see that the world is already full of the glory of God, and that it will one day be filled yet fuller'.[12] Discuss the place of the imagination in rekindling our worship of God for all God is worth.

4. To be made in 'the image of God' (Genesis 1.26) is now commonly thought to convey the idea of the *human role* in creation rather than the *human capacities* (whether intellectual, moral or spiritual). Share ways in which you personally are seeking to reflect the 'image of God' by responding to the ecological crisis.

Prayer

O God, gladly we live and move and have our being in you. Yet always in the midst of this creation-glory, we see sin's shadow and feel death's darkness; around us in the earth, sea and sky, the abuse of matter; beside us in the broken, the hungry and the poor, the betrayal of one another; and often deep within us, a striving against your Spirit.

O Trinity of Love, forgive us that we may forgive one another; heal us that we may be people of healing; and renew us that we also may be makers of peace, in the name of Jesus Christ, who broke down the walls of death and division. Amen

---

12 In a lecture entitled, *The Bible and Christian Imagination*, given at Seattle Pacific University, May 18, 2005

2. The Story of the Fall

The Old Testament never refers to the event described in Genesis 3 as 'the fall'. In fact, one of the earliest references to the term being used comes in the book of 2 Esdras written about AD 100 and included in some Greek versions of the Bible:

> O Adam, what have you done?
> Your sin was not your fall alone;
> it was ours also, the fall of all your descendants (2 Esdras 7.118).[1]

Later, early Church theologians, particularly the Latin fathers, popularized the idea of 'the fall' and gave it prominence in subsequent theological reflection.

In referring to 'the fall' as the second act in the unfolding panoramic Biblical drama the implication is that it was an historical event. Precisely in what way it is to be considered historical is not easy to define but the whole of the biblical narrative makes it clear that something happened that altered things in a way that human beings could not reverse. There is a fundamental dislocation of creation. Creation now bears a tragic wound. John Walton observes that:

> The Old Testament as a whole does not give retrospective information about what we call 'the fall'. Once the events are reported in Genesis 3, no further reference is made to those events or to their ramifications. If we were working from the Old Testament alone, there would be a lot of flexibility concerning how we thought about the entrance and spread of sin.[2]

He goes on to point out how different the situation is in the New Testament:

> The New Testament views the reality of sin and its resulting need for redemption as having entered at a single point in time (punctiliar) through a specific event in time and space. Furthermore,

---

1 Translation from *The New English Bible With Apocrypha.*

Paul correlates that punctiliar event with a corresponding act of redemption: the death of Christ with its resulting atonement – also a punctiliar event.[3]

Paul here treats Adam and Christ as archetypes, representing, on the one hand, all who have sinned and, on the other hand, all who are saved.

> For since death (came) through a human being, the resurrection of the dead has also (come) through a human being; for as all die in Adam, so all (will be) made alive in Christ (1 Corinthians 15.21,22). All are embodied in the one and counted as having participated in the acts of that one.[4]

At this point, Tom Wright warns of a danger. He says,

> The question generated by the scientific study of cosmic and human origins ('did Adam exist?' or 'was there an original Adam?') has become muddled up with a *soteriological* question, as to whether an 'original Adam' is necessary for a biblical doctrine of salvation.[5]

These are important questions and I do not intend to address them here, except to say that, whatever view is taken of an 'historic fall', the Genesis narrative, as we shall note several times, doesn't tell us about the origins of evil. That remains a deep mystery. While there may have been a 'beginning' of sin, no origin or cause is given. What we do know is that human life is lived under the shadow of what might have been. It is not as it should be, not as God intended. There is a gone-wrongness about us and the entire cosmos. We 'have become paradoxically the glory and the garbage of the universe'.[6] We are 'glorious ruins' – 'glorious' because we have been created in God's image but 'ruins' because of our innate propensity to do wrong.

Immediately after the call to work and take care of creation, the man and woman are told by God of the one limit on their existence:

---

3 John H. Walton, *The Lost World Of Adam And Eve*, (IVP, 2015), 102, 103
4 Op.cit., 75
5 Op.cit., 172
6 Graham A. Cole, *God the Peacemaker*, (IVP, 2009), 229

You are free to eat from any tree in the garden; but you must not eat from the tree of the knowledge of good and evil, for when you eat from it you will certainly die (Genesis 2:16,17).

At this juncture a key antagonist enters the biblical story in the form of a highly intelligent talking snake. There is something very elusive and mysterious about the origin of this 'quasi-personal' figure, usually identified with satan in the light of New Testament passages such as the following:

The God of peace will shortly crush satan under your feet (Romans 16.20).

The great dragon was thrown down, that ancient serpent, who is called the devil and satan, the deceiver of the whole world – he was thrown down to earth, and his angels were thrown down with him (Revelation 12.9).

Then I saw an angel coming down from heaven, holding in his hand the key to the bottomless pit and a great chain. He seized the dragon, that ancient serpent, who is the devil and satan, and bound him for a thousand years (Revelation 20.1,2).

Just as the origin of sin is not described in the Bible so too it is silent about how the devil, whom Jesus called the 'father of lies' (John 8:44), came to exist. No explanation is ever given. What the Bible does make clear is that the devil was defeated at the midpoint or epicentre of God's saving plan by the death of Jesus, *Christus Victor*.[7] But pressure to do evil does not come from the devil alone. There are other factors at work causing original humanity to think and act in a corrupt manner. Tom Wright has discerned what he calls a 'three tier perspective' on evil in the Genesis account.[8]

First, as just mentioned, there is evil as the work of satan who predates the human revolt; *second*, there is evil in the form of revolt within the heart of each individual; and *third*, there is systemic evil in human institutions and in the environment.

---

7 See for example, Hebrews 2.14,15 and Colossians 2.15
8 N.T.Wright, *Evil and the Justice of God*, (SPCK, 2006), 23

Evil as the work of satan[9]

This first tier of evil was probably not as evident to the ancient Israelite readers as it is to Tom Wright. John Walton (a good friend of Wright) points out that the ancient Israelite storyteller had 'a far less developed idea of satan than what we find in the New Testament'. The serpent-spoiler in the garden was simply one of 'the wild animals the Lord God had made' (Genesis 3.1). In communicating to an Israelite audience the writer did not identify the talking snake with satan. That came much later.[10] For the first readers of Genesis it was the *consequences* rather than the *agent* which was of particular significance.

There are some Christians who have a paranoid spirituality, which sees evil spirits everywhere, even recognizing them by name as the 'spirit of nicotine' or the 'demon of drink'. When they are questioned about this they are likely to see within the questioner the 'spirit of criticism'. At a conference in the USA a speaker decided to have a mass deliverance of the 'spirit of masturbation' and asked for Kleenex tissues to be given to all the young men present. When the words of exorcism were pronounced, the men were expected to cough up the troublesome demon! It is hard to know whether to laugh or cry when we hear about such extreme accounts of direct satanic encounter.

At the other extreme, there are many Christians in the West influenced by science and trained to deal with the empirical world in naturalistic terms, who exclude the level of satanic evil as part of the realm of fairies, trolls and mythical beings. Western Christians are less likely to see demons as external beings 'flapping around in the air' than as internal forces that afflict the psyche. According to this view, Jesus' struggle with the devil in the temptation narrative was not a struggle with a supernormal demon 'out there'. It is a mythological account expressing a powerful truth that transcends any 'literalist' understanding. Jesus' struggle was with egotism. In psychological terms, the devil represents the ego and its desires.[11] Interpreting the New Testament references to satan, angels

9 I prefer not to use a capital letter for this word.
10 See for example, 1 Chronicles 21
11 This approach is elaborated by David Tacey in *Beyond literal Belief: Religion as*

or evil spirits as though they are actual paranormal beings is analogous, so it is claimed, to a child believing in fairies. It is part of the murky world of superstition from which the Enlightenment has delivered us. The enlightened person understands all such references as myth and psycho-drama. For all practical purposes life today is lived by many Christians as though there are only two realms of persons: God and us. This reduced view of the world has been aptly described as 'the flaw of the excluded middle.'[12] The middle world of unseen spirits, good and bad, has been excluded. Perhaps there is a need to rehabilitate the devil! Charles Sherlock, an Australian theologian, stresses the importance of being clear what the Bible does and does not say about satanic evil. He has observed how restrained the Scriptures are in speaking about satan. He says:

> The struggle in which Christians are involved is not fundamentally negative (against evil), but positive, to do the will of God in a fallen creation.[13]

Certainly, the devil is likened to a roaring lion on the prowl, to be resisted (1Peter 5.8,9) but the struggle is not so much about being warlike (as seen in many western government responses to evil). It is about trusting in the power of Christ.

This positive side of the battle is evident in the way in which some Christians have decided to respond to the horrific terrorist executions carried out by Daesh (the Arabic equivalent of Islamic State). They recognize that in this tormented world we are 'not merely dealing with flesh and blood, but with principalities, and powers and spiritual wickedness in high places' (Ephesians 6.12). The terrorists themselves are often well-educated people who come from middle-class communities. It is clear that education and improved living conditions are not going to alter their behaviour.

Metaphor (Garratt, 2015), 159 - 164

12 P.G. Hiebert, *Anthropological Reflections on Missiological Issues*, (Grand Rapids: Baker, 1994), 189

13 Charles Sherlock, *The Overcoming of Satan* Grove Spirituality No 17

Most of the media discussion on the Syrian refugee crisis has been about the management of displaced people, and dealing with the human agents of the suffering, rather than looking with the eye of Scripture-informed faith on the spiritual root of the problem. By taking seriously the New Testament teaching about the spiritual warfare in which Christians are engaged and the need for positive action and focused prayer, a website called, 'Adopt a Terrorist for Prayer' has been established. It includes the profiles of a large number of terrorists and insightful suggestions as to how to pray for them. This is one way of acting positively on Jesus' instruction: 'love your enemies and *pray for those who persecute you*' (Matthew 5.44). As Andrew Symes from Anglican Mainstream has written:

> The informed Christian response is more than an expression of solidarity that comes from shared humanity, or a recital of political analysis; it should certainly be very cautious about supporting military actions. What is needed is serious intercession which involves unmasking and naming the terrifying presence behind Daesh/ISIS, corrupt governments and the furious persecution directed at the church in the Middle East.[14]

This kind of intercession represents an important challenge for today's Christian communities to rise above their own negative feelings towards those who are caught in the dark, satanic evil of terrorism and actually make a positive response by praying for them. This first dark tier of evil has been nowhere more clearly and biblically recognized than in the words of C.S. Lewis writing in the preface of 'The Screwtape Letters'. He astutely remarks:

> There are two equal and opposite errors into which our race can fall about devils. One is to disbelieve in their existence. The other is to believe, and to feel an excessive and unhealthy interest in them. They themselves are equally pleased by both errors and hail a materialist or a magician with the same delight.[15]

14 See Andrew Symes, *'Things fall apart: Yeats' sphinx and the need for spiritual warfare'*, September 8th, 2015, Anglican Mainstream web site.
15 C. S. Lewis, *The Screwtape Letters*, 1942, Collins Fount, 9

Evil as the revolt of individuals

An old proverb goes to the nub of the human predicament in declaring that 'the heart of the human problem is the problem of the human heart'. Paul struggles with his own inner dividedness and the gravitational pull of sin, when he cries out:

> I do not understand my own actions. For I do not do what I want, but I do the very thing I hate. ... I can will what is right, but I cannot do it. For I do not do the good I want, but the evil I do not want is what I do (Romans 7.15,18,19).

Genesis 2 and 3 portray the frustration of God's creation purpose in a sequence of stories that together show how wrongdoing came to dominate the human story. Rowan Williams has suggested that the nearest thing that these early chapters of Genesis come to in describing what actually happened in the fall is that there was a contravening of a command, a refusal to listen.[16] This story is about the way *not* listening to God sets off a chain reaction. It affects relationships between people and God, between men and women, between human beings and their vocation, and between human beings and their world.

The habitual activity of the devil is to lie about the word of God and so destroy faith in the truthfulness and trustworthiness of God's Word so that people no longer listen to God. The same tactic was played out in the desert when satan tempted our Lord by distorting the word of God as the very point of assault. But Jesus refused to listen to the voice of the devil. In that contest, he immediately reversed the temptation to which the man and the woman in the Genesis story yielded. There were plenty of trees in the garden from which they could eat fruit but they were forbidden to eat from 'the tree of the knowledge of good and evil'. It represented a kind of sacrament of death. Instead of listening to God they chose to listen to the demonic suggestion that in setting limitations, God was deliberately impoverishing life, whispering in their ears: 'Why not please yourself? Don't let God's boundaries curb

---

16 See Rowan Williams, *Being Christian: Baptism, Bible, Eucharist, Prayer*, (SPCK, 2014) 21

your freedom. True satisfaction can be found in what God forbids'. Their refusal to listen to God's word amounts to a desire to be quit of God, that is, to be autonomous. For them, ethics is no longer reflective of any objective moral order that lies beyond personal preference. It is a matter of 'historical happenstance'. As a popular doggerel puts it:

It all depends on where you are,
It all depends on who you are,
It all depends on what you feel,
It all depends on how you feel.
It all depends on how you're raised,
It all depends on what is praised,
What's right today is wrong tomorrow,
Joy in France, in England sorrow.
It all depends on point of view,
Australia or Timbuctoo,
In Rome do as the Romans do.
If tastes just happen to agree
Then you have morality.
But where there are conflicting trends,
It all depends, it all depends … [17]

Graham Tomlin's comment draws out the consequences of the human refusal to listen to God and to obey God's word: 'When the fruit of the tree of knowledge is eaten, a pattern of addiction sets in, and a web of behaviour settles, in which it becomes impossible to kick the habit of independence'.[18]

The story continues with the 'blame game' whereby the blame is shifted to get away from the voice of conscience.

The Lord God said, "Have you eaten of the tree of which I commanded you not to eat?" The man said, "The woman you gave to be with me, she gave me fruit from the tree, and I ate". Then the Lord God said to the woman, "What is this that you have done?" The woman said, "the serpent tricked me, and I ate" (3:11-13).

17 Quoted by John Stott, *The Radical Disciple*, (IVP, 2010), 24
18 Op.cit., Tomlin, 94

In this passage, we see the typical human search for a scapegoat in order to shirk the necessity of repentance. It is the great evasion of the so-called victim culture, where we are all victims and no-one is responsible any more. The Genesis story recognizes an ultimate divine accountability. It conveys a sense of a moral universe presided over by God. The desire for autonomy makes the self the ultimate authority. Bishop Peter Jensen has pointed to a curious quirk in fallen human nature when he says:

> Even in a world in which we no longer believe in judgement, we manage to both criticise each other, and also to refuse to agree that we ourselves are guilty. Despite what we say with our lips, we behave for all the world as though the universe is built on the principle that there is a judgement day.[19]

Adam and Eve experience a foretaste of Judgement Day when they are expelled from the Garden of Eden. Yet, even then, God continues with fallen humanity in its brokenness and its cast-out-ness. Banished from the garden they are denied access to the 'tree of life', doomed to die. They are mortal - 'dust you are and to dust you shall return'.

At the personal level, evil is seen in every human life. In his raw, in-your-face book, Francis Spufford talks about human sin and failure as HPtFtu – the 'human propensity to fuck things up'.[20] Alexander Solzhenitsyn makes the same point with a little more refinement:

> The line between good and evil doesn't run between me and you, or us and them. It runs clean down the centre of every heart.[21]

Sin affects every part of our being including our minds. All human thought is both fallen and finite. Our thinking isn't as detached and objective as we sometimes think. Only God apprehends perfectly and certainly. Ashley Null summarises Thomas Cranmer's understanding of human nature when he says, 'What the heart loves, the will chooses and the mind justifies'.[22] John Stackhouse recommends that:

---

19 Peter Jensen, Studies for Lent and Other Times, Power & Promise, 2014, APA, 24
20 Ibid, 27
21 Alexander Solzhenitsyn, The Gulag Archipelago, 1918 – 1956, (1973)
22 Ashley Null, Thomas Cranmer's Theology of the Heart, Trinity Journal for Theology

Instead of simply saying we believe or don't believe this or that – or, worse, simply asserting this or that, - it would be a good discipline for ourselves and more helpful communication to others to begin more sentences with "It seems to me that ..." or "As I understand it ...," to indicate our awareness that we are not delivering the simple truth of the matter.[23]

As well as our inability to reason effectively and wisely, our emotions, desires, morals and sexuality have been affected by the fall. Dr Sean Doherty has suggested that it would be helpful in the debates over sexuality in our Church if we avoided using labels like 'straight' because 'nobody has a 'straight' sexuality in the sense of a 'normal' or 'healthy' one. Nobody's sexuality remains unaffected by the fall – there is no moral high ground.[24]

The consequences of the story of the fall are not confined to chapters 2 and 3 of Genesis. The ravages of sin unfold further in chapters 4 to 11 where the third level of the three tier perspective on evil begins to emerge, namely, systemic evil.

Evil as the work of institutions

The virus of sin cannot be quarantined. As an old proverb puts it: 'you can bring a pig into the parlour, but that doesn't change the pig: though it certainly changes the parlour'. The cascading consequences of the primordial disobedience are manifold and spread from Eden to Babel, infiltrating and infecting human relationships and spilling over into the ecological system. To quote Spufford again, 'there's a crack in everything. ... The vision is of an intrinsically imperfect cosmos, hairlined through and through with flaws, chipped and battered and patched'.[25]

The original human refusal to live within limits is re-enacted by our contemporary wastefulness. Commenting on this, Patricia K. Tull sums

and Ministry 1, 2007, 30
23 John Stackhouse, *Need to Know*, (Oxford University Press, 2014), 211
24 Sean Doherty, Anvil, 30, March, 2014
25 Ibid, 47

up the consequences well when she says the 'quality of the soul' affects the 'quality of the soil'.[26]

The Lord God said: cursed is the ground because of you; in toil you shall eat of it all the days of your life; thorns and thistles it shall bring forth for you (Genesis. 3:17b,18a).

In the final chapter of his book *A Short History of Nearly Everything*, Bill Bryson refers to the extraordinary wanton destructiveness of human beings. Although he makes no explicit reference to a Creator, he provides the raw materials for the Christian understanding of the human condition when he writes:

If you were designing an organism to look after life in our lonely cosmos, to monitor where it is going and keep a record of where it has been, you wouldn't choose human beings for the job. But here's an extremely salient point: we have been chosen, by fate or providence or whatever you wish to call it. As far as we can tell, we are the best there is. We may be all there is. It's an unnerving thought that we may be the living universe's supreme achievement and its worst nightmare simultaneously.[27]

According to John Goldingay, 'Genesis portrays the world in an Armenian or Nazi or Rwandan or Darfur state'.[28] Evil reached such a level that God resolved to send a flood as an act of 'un-creation' and to start all over again having first wiped out 'all flesh', except for the family of Noah and a pair of all creatures. In the words of John Dominic Crossan, 'What began with Cain killing Abel escalated from humanity to divinity with God killing Earth.'[29] Although Crossan understands these stories in terms of the literary genre of parable, he nevertheless has an expectation that they will provide sophisticated metaphysical answers to the way in which divine action and human responsibility

---

26 Patricia K. Tull, *Inhabiting Eden: Christians, the Bible, and the Ecological Crisis*, (Westminster John Knox, 2013), 43
27 Bill Bryson, *A Short History of Nearly Everything*, (Black Swan, UK, 2003), 572
28 John Goldingay, *Genesis for Everyone: Part 1, chapters 1 – 16*, (SPCK, 2010), 95
29 John Dominic Crossan, *How To Read The Bible & Still Be A Christian*, (HarperOne, 2015), 70

are related. For him, the flood story presents God as a divine terrorist who 'has been sucked completely into humanity's escalatory violence'. John Goldingay also reads the Genesis stories as parables, but he has no expectation that they will provide answers to the *why's and wherefore's* of God's ways. We can ask the questions but there are no final answers. God's providential ways are inscrutable. Goldingay readily acknowledges that two questions are provoked by the violence of the flood story. We might ask 'what kind of God allows this to happen?' and we might also ask, 'what kind of creatures are human beings that we should cause and allow this to happen?' He writes:

> If global warming causes some terrible catastrophe engulfing the human and the animal world, we will be able to see it in regular cause-effect terms. We will be a little relieved not to have to reckon that God had deliberately made it happen by an act of judgment. On the other hand, people will certainly be asking, "Why did God allow this?" The Bible is capable of seeing catastrophes in cause-effect terms, and something of this nature is implied in the way the story keeps using the word "devastate." Devastation issues in devastation, as would be the case in global warming. Humanity has devastated its way and devastated the world, so God will devastate humanity and devastate the world. Yet the Bible is also tough-minded about attributing such catastrophes to God's direct action. Stuff happens; and sometimes, at least, God not merely lets it happen but makes it happen.[30]

The questions are asked but they cannot be resolved satisfactorily. Crossan maintains a sharp distinction between God's 'distributive justice' and human civilization's 'retributive justice'. He is convinced that 'retributive justice' can have no place in God's dealing with humanity. Biblical stories such as the flood cannot possibly reflect the truth of God's action. Such stories are unfair. Goldingay agrees that these stories portray God as being unfair. But he then goes on to claim that they fit with the rest of the way life works. He says:

---

30 John Goldingay, *Genesis for Everyone: Part 1, chapters 1 – 16*, (SPCK, 2010), 100

God does not give everyone equal gifts, capacities, and lengths of life. God did not decide to make humanity equal. Life is not fair. The priority in God's mind is not fairness but how we serve God and serve other people with the gifts, capacities, and lengths of life that God gives us.[31]

What matters in this brilliantly blended account is the immensely rich theological point of God's covenant. Later covenants in the Bible are bilateral, as in a marriage covenant which assumes that two people are making a mutual commitment. This first covenant with Noah is a unilateral, unconditional promise. *'Never again'* will God exterminate humans or animate creation (Genesis 9.11). There is a 'gone-wrongness' in humanity that continues to impact all creation. But because of God's *'never again'* promise, life can go on without fear of ultimate annihilation. Genesis 1-11 traces the spread of sin alongside the continuing evidence of blessing. 'Noah found favour (grace) in the sight of the Lord' (Genesis 6.8). Perhaps the joker had a point when he claimed that it was Noah who became the greatest financier in the Bible because he floated his stock while everyone else was in liquidation! Throughout the rest of the human story, sin continues but so too does God's grace.

The tower of Babel story (Genesis 11.1-9) wraps up the opening chapters. It starts again with a group from the east and a single language. They too soon succumb to the basic temptation that faced the man and the woman in the Garden of Eden. The human desire to assert independence by mastery over the world is now seen on a large social scale in the building of the tower of Babel. The Creator turns the gift of language by which humans communicate into a confusing babel.

At the corporate or systemic level 'there begins to emerge a lack of goodness that is somehow greater than the sum lack in the individuals'. At this point it almost seems as if evil can take on a life of its own without it necessarily consisting of anything'.[32] We see this systemic

---

31 Ibid, Goldingay, 100
32 Stephen Torr, *A Dramatic Pentecostal/Charismatic Anti-Theodicy*, (Pickwick

evil in the corrupt religious and political systems that opposed Jesus. All of our institutions require independent checks and balances to ensure probity and transparency, especially where power and money are involved. Systemic evil represents a repetition of the eating from the tree of the knowledge of good and evil performed on a grand scale. In corporate governance - whether in the church, politics or sport – there will always be a role for the whistle-blower.

Waleed Aly writing in *The Age* newspaper described 2014 as a year which felt 'positively, gallingly crappy'.[33] It included personal acts of terrorism, aviation crashes and the Ebola virus. 'Those catastrophic, unthinkable, bizarrely tragic events panicked, angered and depressed many Australian people'. His words conveyed the notion behind this third tier of evil. We feel overwhelmed by an evil and corruption that has infiltrated all our biological, ecological, political, religious and sociological systems. The flaws in creation have been likened to a glitch in a computer program as a result of a virus. The resultant havoc causes flaws and faults to appear whenever the program is run. This means that while we should always be horrified by evil, we should never be surprised by it.

The triple tiers of sin discerned by Tom Wright in the Genesis story suggest that its origin is complex and may be satanic; or the desire for personal autonomy; or the permeation of dark, systemic evil; or as is more likely, a combination of one or other of these three tiers. In fact, personal sin nearly always has social dimensions. As the early chapters of Genesis make clear, there is no way in which the individual can keep sin contained within.

Throughout Genesis 1-11 the story-teller provides explanations of the origins for various features of human life, known technically as aetiologies. The origin of the pain of childbirth is attributed to Eve's disobedience (Genesis 3.16); the origin of the arts and crafts is attributed to the ingenuity of two characters, Jubal and Tubal-cain

Publications, 2013) 137,138
33 The Age, Friday, January 9, 2015

(Genesis 4.21,22); and the diverse human languages originate from God's scattering of the people after the building of the tower of Babel (Genesis 11.1-9). But as we have seen, the aetiology of sin remains unclear. Charles Sherlock emphasizes this point when he says:

> A great deal is therefore at stake for Christian faith in the way we understand sin and its beginning. It is important to note that to speak of the 'beginning' of sin is not the same as identifying an 'origin', which remains a profound riddle: 'They hated me without a cause' (John 15.25). Why human beings, created in the image of God, should reject their Creator (then and now) makes no sense, but to look for a 'cause' external to ourselves implies that it lies somewhere else in creation, implying either cosmic dualism, or that creation was made evil, both rejected in the Scriptures. Further, such a search encourages human beings to look for a scapegoat outside of themselves, and thus to shirk the necessity of repentance; this was precisely the initial reaction of Adam and Eve in Eden (Genesis 3.12-13).[34]

For me personally, the more pressing daily problem is not where sin comes from so much as what to do with it as it lurks just beneath the surface of my life threatening to erupt. Many people today fear that to involve oneself in self-examination by raking over failings and brooding over shortcomings a person can get sucked into morbid introspection and depression. In view of this perceived danger, they adopt a relentlessly upbeat and cheerful attitude to life, prayer and worship regardless of the state of their relationship with God. Alternatively, they may adopt the ego-centric happiness track offered by pop psychology. The whole notion of 'sin' as dishonouring and defying God is avoided. Those who inhabit this self-world look only for therapy, not for forgiveness or the regenerating work of the Holy Spirit. Bishop Stephen Cottrell has jokingly suggested that he'd like to write a book entitled, 'Come back sin. All is forgiven'.

But if some people have problems because they refuse to look honestly at their lives other people can have problems because they keep looking

---

34 Charles Sherlock, *The Doctrine of Humanity*, (IVP, 1996) 63

at their lives in order to refuel their resentment or guilt. Instead of focusing on the road ahead they keep on staring in the rear-view mirror defining themselves by their regrets and crash again and again. What is necessary in either case is that things get dealt with as we go along and that nothing is left to accumulate and fester. Forgiveness is a creative act. It is in exposing our wounds that the Spirit comes. The wise person recognizes that: 'God uses self-examination not to hurt us but to help us "find where it hurts" so that wounds can be dressed and healed'.[35] We often fail to grasp the nature of forgiveness because we have such a pitifully weak grasp of the extent to which we are loved by God. We live our lives saying that God loves us but behaving as if we are convinced that he is out to get us. If we hide from the objectionable and obnoxious parts of our lives and refuse to take them with us in prayer, God cannot work in us and gradually change us into his likeness. God doesn't want us to pretend. I love the honesty of a short prayer used by an Anglican nun, Mother Mary Clare. It is one sentence: 'Here I am Lord, what a mess'. God can live with the reality of the mess and muddle in our lives, even if we find it hard to do so!

Questions for reflection

1. Liberal Christians tend to focus on the systemic evil that permeates the social fabric through such evils as economic inequities, racial prejudice, gender bias and a spoiled, sick creation. Conservative Christians tend to focus on personal sin and the need for relationship with God. Would this polarization in the Christian community be helped if systemic evil was regarded as a *symptom* and personal sin as the *cause*?

2. Do you think that those who take the satanic realm seriously have entered the realm of fantasy?

3. Daily our Newspapers and TV news give reports of terror and violence. It is little wonder that fear invades our souls. But should we be surprised by these reports? What are we Christians to do about the fact that our world is beautiful? What are we Christians to do about the fact that our world is ugly?

---

35 Julia Gatta & Martin Smith, *Go in Peace*, (Canterbury Press, 2013), 68

4. Much preaching today offers no real summons to self-examination and repentance. The judgment theme of the gospels is reduced to nil and the invitation to share in the Eucharist is distorted into 'cheap grace'. Do you think that perhaps Bishop Stephen Cottrell has a point when he jokingly says, 'bring back sin - all is forgiven'.

5. Because of sin, our delight in the wonder of creation is often fleeting or mingled with pain or sorrow. How does that statement line up with your experience?

Prayer

Gracious God, our sins are too heavy to carry, too real to hide, and too deep to undo. Forgive what our lips tremble to name, what our hearts can no longer bear, and what has become for us a consuming fire of judgment. Set us free from a past that we cannot change; open to us a future in which we can be changed; and grant us grace to grow more and more in your likeness and image, through Jesus Christ, the light of the world. Amen[36]

---

36 Quoted by Brian McLaren in *Finding Our Way Again: The Return Of The Ancient Practice*, (Thomas Nelson, 2008), 109

3. THE STORY OF ISRAEL

More and more people today are opting for a kind of cocktail approach to religion - 'religion a' la carte'. Picking from a smorgasbord of religious varieties they choose what happens to suit them at the time, and leave the rest alone. For them, the letters, G.O.D may refer to Yahweh or Allah, or Brahman or any of the other names given to an infinite, universal, deity.

For many people, the *particular* religions associated with these infinite, universal, realities are not important. They are *particular*, culturally determined paths, whether Judaism, Christianity, Islam, Hinduism or Buddhism but all lead ultimately to the same *universal* reality. One is as good as the other. In Australia, immigration and multicultural policies have led to religious diversity as the new normal. Other religions are accepted as being at least as valid as Christianity. Many 'New Age' people adopt a 'pick and mix' attitude in relation to these religions whereby 'you float your own boat'. Your truth is true for you and my truth is true for me.

But the Bible, which is the text in which the Christian faith recognizes its 'title deeds', contests this 'cocktail', relativist approach to religion. Whereas many people today are only interested in the existence of a *universal* reality and are indifferent or opposed to the *particular* form it takes, in the Bible the *universal* and the *particular* coincide. God discloses Godself in the Scriptures as the *universal* 'Creator of heaven and earth' and the *particular* 'God of Abraham, Isaac and Jacob'. Most spectacularly, God is made known in the *particular* first century Jew, Jesus. In his brilliant little book, *Bible and Mission: Christian Witness in a Postmodern World*, Richard Bauckham develops the implications of this special understanding of the relationship between the *particular* and the *universal* for the entire Biblical story.

Central to God's identity throughout the Bible is that God is a sending God and this sending is never aimless. It always expresses God's love in a sending movement from the *particular* to the *universal*. Election, whether of an individual or of a nation, is a characteristic of divine activity throughout the Bible. God's tendency to be selective is something that many Christians often feel embarrassed about. It appears to be discriminatory and can easily tip over into an exclusivist ideology. This is what happened to Israel in the middle of the 8th century BCE. The nation used its special sense of being called by God as a warrant for self-indulgence. The prophet Amos challenged this smug sense of what Walter Brueggemann refers to as Israel's sense of *'only-ness'*.

> Hear this word that the Lord has spoken against you, O people of Israel, against the whole family that I brought up out of the land of Egypt: *You only* have I known of all the families of the earth; therefore I will punish you for all your iniquities (Amos 3.1,2).

According to the prophet Amos, to be 'chosen' is to be exposed to greater judgment not less. It is complacent and hypocritical believers who have most to fear from God's judgement. Amos declared that the hoped-for 'Day of the Lord' would be the black day of divine judgment (Amos 5.18-20). Externally, at its mid-point, 8th century Israel was prosperous and confident of the future. Inwardly, it was toxic. Insofar as there was any hope for the future it was on the condition that justice would be practised:

> Take away from me the noise of your songs; I will not listen to the melody of your harps. But let justice roll down like waters, and righteousness like an ever-flowing stream (Amos 5.23,24).

At its best human love is a response to God's love, a response that leads to action as God's beloved seek to live out the implications of their grateful answering love. God's election must be linked with inclusiveness not exclusiveness, if it is not to be dismissed as callous and unfair. John Goldingay gives a homely illustration of how this may be the case when he writes:

> A friend recently wrote to my wife and me and ended 'with all my love'. This might seem hard on her husband and sons. Yet there

can be something about love that makes it not necessarily exhaust itself when given wholly to one person; it can mysteriously self-regenerate and multiply in the giving so that it pours out over others than the original object.[1]

The closest that the Old Testament comes to providing an answer to the grounds for God's choosing can be found in Deuteronomy 7.7,8:

> It was not because you were more numerous than any other people that the Lord set his heart on you – for you were the fewest of all peoples. It was because the Lord loved you and kept the oath that he swore to your ancestors, that the Lord has brought you out with a mighty hand, and redeemed you from the house of slavery, from the hand of Pharaoh King of Egypt.

God's choice cannot be ascribed to any of Israel's attributes, whether its size, holiness or potential. Rather God's choice is grounded in the mystery of the divine love and faithfulness.

Bauckham illustrates God's election purposes with three major 'flight passages' from the *particular* to the *universal* which make up the long, unfolding 'backstory'[2] of mission in the first Testament. He summarises these three trajectories as follows:

> God's purpose begins with a singular choice: God singles out first, Abraham, then Israel, then David. The three movements that begin with these three choices by God each have their own distinctive theme, one aspect of God's purpose for the world.[3]

Blessing: from Abraham to all nations

The paradigmatic instance of God's plan of election is the choice of Abraham to be a blessing to the rest of humanity. The Creator God's blessing on humankind to 'be fruitful and multiply' (Genesis 1.28) now becomes a threefold promise to Abraham. God will make his

---

1 John Goldingay, *Key Questions about Christian Faith – Old Testament Answers*, (Baker Academic, 2010), 213
2 Tom Wright uses the descriptor of *'backstory'* in reference to the Old Testament metanarrative. See 'Simply Good News, 3
3 Op, cit, 27

descendants a great nation; God will give to his descendants a land of their own and God will bring blessing to all the families of the earth through his descendants:

> Now the Lord said to Abram, "Go from your country and your kindred and your father's house to the land that I will show you. I will make of you a great nation, and I will bless you, and make your name great, so that you will be a blessing. I will bless those who bless you, and the one who curses you I will curse; and in you all the families of the earth shall be blessed" (Genesis 12.1-3).

Clearly, God's choice of Abraham is not without rhyme or reason. It is the outworking of God's love and God's desire to bless all people. One person is chosen as a means of blessing for all.

The anonymous prophet in Babylon, known as Second Isaiah, encouraged the exiles in the sixth century BCE by echoing this promise of blessing and exhorting them not to forget this ancient tradition, which goes back to God's promise to Abraham:

> Look to the rock from which you were hewn, to the quarry from which you were dug. Look to Abraham your father and to Sarah who bore you, for he was but one when I called him, but I blessed him and made him many (Isaiah 51:2).

Isaiah is following the first trajectory - from one particular man, Abraham, a blessing will flow out to many.

Today, the word 'blessing' tends to be used by all sorts of people to refer, in a vague sort of way, to wishing people well. But, as Bauckham explains, 'in the Bible it characteristically describes God's provision for human flourishing.'[4] It refers to God's generous and abundant giving. In addition, Bauckham points out that blessing must be seen as relational. To be blessed by God is not only to know God's gifts but to know God in God's excessive giving.

---

4 Op, cit, 34

The movement of blessing is a movement that goes out from God and returns to God. Those who experience the blessing of God in turn bless God which means that they give all that creatures really can give to God: thanksgiving and praise.[5]

Whenever we thank God for his gifts, we enjoy them doubly, both in the initial experience and in our gratitude. Now fast forward to Paul's letter to the Galatians in the New Testament. There we find Paul hopping on the same trajectory of 'blessing' and giving it a Christological twist. Writing about the seed of Abraham, the Messiah, he says,

> Christ (the Messiah) redeemed us from the curse of the law by becoming a curse for us …in order that in Christ Jesus the blessing of Abraham might come to the Gentiles (Gal. 3:13-14).

The blessing promised to Abraham ultimately trumps the curse mentioned in the early chapters of Genesis, through the saving death of Christ, and so flows out to all people. The 'flight path' of the three-fold promise to a particular individual, Abraham, is part of God's great plan to bring about God's desire for relationship with people of all nations so that they and the entire creation will flourish.

Revelation: from Israel to all nations

The book of Exodus is concerned with how God singles out a *particular* group of people who are the descendants of Abraham. God chose the small, nomadic nation of Israel from the rest of humankind for a special, demanding vocation, to be a kingdom of priests. Once again, we find that 'out of the whole, God chooses a part'.

At the giving of the law at Mount Sinai, God says:

> You yourselves have seen what I did in Egypt, and how I carried you on eagles' wings and brought you to myself. Now if you obey me fully and keep my covenant, then out of all the nations you will be my treasured possession. Although the whole earth is mine, you will be for me a kingdom of priests and a holy nation (Exodus.19.4-6).

---

5 Op.cit, 34

God's purpose in choosing Israel to be a kingdom of priests was so that they might see their vocation as having a universal revelation of God for the nations. Over and over again in the Exodus narrative we hear the refrain - 'for the sake of God's own name' or 'to make God's name renowned through all the earth'. God tells Moses that he will harden Pharaoh's heart so that he can multiply the awesome signs in order that 'the Egyptians shall know that I am the Lord' (Exod. 7:5). Then through Moses, God tells Pharaoh that this is the chief reason for the dramatic acts of judgment upon the land of Egypt:

> Then the Lord said to Moses, "Go to Pharaoh; for I have hardened his heart and the heart of his officials, in order that I may show these signs of mine among them, and that you may tell your children and grandchildren how I made fools of the Egyptians and what signs I have done among them – so that you may know that I am the Lord" (Exod. 10:1,2).

The culminating event of luring the Egyptians into the Sea of Reeds (not the Red Sea as is commonly supposed) and their consequent destruction is likewise seen as a manifestation of God's awesome power and glory:

> Then I will harden the hearts of the Egyptians so that they will go in after them; and so I will gain glory for myself over Pharaoh and all his army, his chariots, and his chariot drivers. And the Egyptians shall know that I am the Lord, when I have gained glory for myself over Pharaoh, his chariots, and his chariot drivers (Exod. 14:17,18).

God is at centre stage in the Exodus narrative. As Mark Dever has written:

> Exodus directly challenges the idea that God does everything for humanity's sake. Humans *are not* the ultimate purpose of creation. God's own glory is! … The whole book, you could say, is about God establishing his own fame![6]

Many people struggle with the notion of God desiring fame, thinking of it as a form of flattery. It was an issue that troubled a student attending a university mission conducted by Professor David Carson. The student asked:

---

6 Mark Dever, The Message of the Old Testament: Promises Made, 2006, Wheaton: Crossway, 100

In human relationships, we learn to distrust and despise anyone who always wants to be number one, who is offended if he or she is not number one. So why should we not take umbrage at a God who wants to be number one, who is offended if he or she is not number one?[7]

Bauckham contends that the analogy of God's making God's name renowned in all the earth is an analogy which is appropriate uniquely to God. He writes:

For a human being to seek such universal and eternal fame would be to aspire to divinity, but God must desire to be known to be God. The good of God's human creatures requires that he be known to them as God. There is no vanity, only revelation of truth, in God's demonstrating of God's deity to the nations.[8]

Graham Cole offers an additional explanation for this apparent divine narcissism. He considers the problem in the context of the doctrine of the Trinity where there is a mutual glorification in the inner life of the triune God. He says:

If the God of the Bible is understood in non-trinitarian terms, then such a goal seems *prima facie* unworthy of God. God is the celestial egotist. However, if God is really triune, that divine dance of mutual love and glorying, then glory is other-person-centred, even within the Godhead.[9]

The mission of one nation to all the other nations is directed to the acknowledgement and worship of the true God and, once again, the apostle Paul writing in the New Testament takes up this trajectory and gives it Christological significance. Writing to the Philippians he extols the glory of the Messiah:

At the name of Jesus every knee should bend, in heaven and on earth and under the earth, and every tongue confess that Jesus Christ is Lord to the glory of God the Father (Phil 2:10).

---

7 Quoted by Graham Cole in *God the Peacemaker*, (IVP, 2009), 227
8 Op, cit, *Bible and Mission*, 37
9 Op.cit., 228

Reading the Old Testament backwards in the light of Jesus we could paraphrase John 3:16 and say, 'God so loved the world that he chose Israel' – not because Israel was better than the surrounding nations. Once again it is the writer of the book of Deuteronomy who makes it clear that Israel had no greater righteousness than the Canaanites:

> Know, then, that the Lord your God is not giving you this good land to occupy because of your righteousness; for you are a stubborn people. Remember and do not forget how you provoked the Lord your God to wrath in the wilderness; you have been rebellious against the Lord from the day you came out of the land of Egypt until you came to this place (Deuteronomy 9.6,7).

In choosing the people of Israel as bearers of the revelation of God's glory and as a light to the nations, God knew full well that Israel was part of the problem. God's ultimate rescue plan, whether from Egypt or Babylon, was not simply political restoration to Jerusalem but restoration to Godself. What Israel needed, towards the end of the Old Testament narrative, was not just the ending of the Babylonian exile but also the forgiveness of their sin. The Persian ruler Cyrus as God's agent could take care of the first by issuing an edict for the Jews to return home from exile in Babylon in three major waves between 538 and 444 BC. Only the 'despised and rejected' suffering servant of the Lord would accomplish the second – the forgiveness of sin (Isaiah 53,3,4). Once again we see that the 'flight path' of God's promise to make the particular nation Israel a 'kingdom of priests', to show forth God's glory and to make God's name known to the nations throws light on Jesus and his priestly work of reconciliation.

Harmony: from David to the whole cosmos

Richard Bauckham has drawn attention to just how pivotal David is in the Biblical narrative when he says,

> That David is a pivotal figure in the story of the whole Bible we can see by the amount of space the Old Testament devotes to telling his story. There are some sixty chapters, which is two-thirds as much

as the New Testament devotes to telling the story of Jesus, eighty-nine chapters in the four Gospels altogether. David's only rival for importance in the Old Testament is Moses, but we do not really get to know Moses in the intimate way we do David. In those sixty chapters David appears in a remarkable number of roles: a shepherd boy, a military hero, a musician and poet, a devoted friend, a lover of several women, an astute politician, a dispenser of justice, a founder of religious institutions, an adulterer and murderer, an indulgent and heart-broken father, and, throughout all of these roles and however paradoxically, a man devoted to God, the king God chose because he was, said God, 'a man after my own heart.'[10]

It remains unclear exactly how David came to prominence but the Old Testament is clear that David was chosen by God to replace Saul and to be the founder of a long line of kings. He united the North and South kingdoms and established his capital in Jerusalem. But his failures are despicable. His manipulative behaviour and adultery with Bathsheba and subsequent murder of her husband is recounted in considerable detail (2 Samuel 11). Despite all of this, the unfolding narrative reveals the God who 'writes straight with crooked lines.' David passes into the tradition as the ideal king.

In a key passage in 2 Samuel, David says to the prophet Nathan: "See now, I am living in a house of cedar, but the ark of God stays in a tent" (2 Samuel 7.2). David therefore proposes that he should build a house, meaning a temple, for God to live in. But the prophet Nathan, acting as God's mouthpiece, responds to David's proposal with a remarkable play-on-words and a counterproposal. Timothy Keller brings out the force of the word play when he writes:

David wanted to build God a house but God said, "No, I will build you a house". God would establish David's royal family line and it would ultimately reveal God's glory in a more permanent, far-reaching, and universal way.[11]

10 From a sermon preached at Trinity College Chapel, Cambridge, 28th October, 2012
11 Timothy Keller, *Prayer: Experiencing Awe and Intimacy with God*, (Hodder & Stoughton, 2014), 64

Acting as God's mouthpiece, the prophet Nathan declares that there will never be lacking an heir to sit upon David's throne:

> Moreover the Lord declares to you that the Lord will make you a house. When your days are fulfilled and you lie down with your ancestors, I will raise up your offspring after you, who shall come forth from your body, and I will establish his kingdom. He shall build a house for my name, and I will establish the throne of his kingdom forever. I will be a father to him, and he shall be a son to me (2 Samuel 7:11b-13).

Is this, Timothy Keller wonders, 'just ancient imperial hyperbole, like "O may the king live forever"?' The Old Testament does sometimes use the term 'eternal' in a less than absolute sense. How can an individual human being reign forever?

The answer to that question comes if we cut to the period just before the Babylonian exile in 587 BCE. In that bleak period, we hear another of God's messengers, the prophet Isaiah[12] preaching a message of hope about God's universal reign through the extraordinary power of one who is more than an ordinary mortal:

> For a child has been born to us, a son given to us; authority rests upon his shoulders; and he is named Wonderful Counsellor, Mighty God, Everlasting Father, Prince of Peace. His authority shall grow continually, and there shall be endless peace for the throne of David and his kingdom. He will establish and uphold it with justice and with righteousness from this time onward and forevermore (Isaiah 9:6,7).

David was succeeded by Solomon. The Old Testament writers extol him as a great and wise king (1Kings 3:12-13 and 1Kings 4.29-34). His final years were problematic and on his death the United Kingdom he inherited from his father David split in two with the ten northern

---

12 Most Old Testament scholars maintain that the book of Isaiah consists of three major collections from different contexts which have been subjected to a long editorial process. So-called 2nd Isaiah (chapters 40 to 55) and 3rd Isaiah (chapters 56 to the end) were probably members of the school of prophets attached to an original founding prophet in Jerusalem (chapters 1 to 39).

tribes of Israel rebelling against the Davidic dynasty. These tribes became known as the kingdom of Israel, while the two southern tribes remaining in unity with the Davidic dynasty became known as the kingdom of Judah. In the long succession of kings that ruled over the divided monarchy, few were noted for ruling 'with justice and with righteousness'. Kings came and went, after assassinating their predecessors and then being assassinated themselves. Again and again the prophets, marching to the beat of a different drum, acted as God's watch-dogs. They struggled for distributive justice (adequacy for all and enough for each) on behalf of the powerless triad in the ancient world; the widow (husbandless), the orphan (fatherless) and the stranger (without family backup). As the inadequacies of the kings were exposed, the hope of a worthy representative for the monarchy grew and gave rise to Messianic prophecies such as those in Isaiah. His words carried a vision of kingship reshaped. Always, the word of the prophet had relevance to the political situation of the day but often there was the kind of 'prophetic overspill' that gave the words a fuller, future application. The fulfilment outstrips local petty monarchs. As Graham Cole has commented:

> A robust doctrine of the inspiration of Scripture does not reduce the text merely to what the human authors intended. There is the divine author. The story of Scripture is a story of double agency. There can be a fuller meaning in canonical perspective that later events clarify.[13]

The 'prophetic overspill' has been likened to a little girl requesting a doll for Christmas that opens and closes her eyes. Instead she receives one that walks and talks and weeps and wets its pants! She does not complain that the doll is not what she had hoped for. She is thrilled with her parent's ability to come up with surprises that more than fulfil her expectations.

The three thematic threads running through the long backstory of the Jewish Bible all converge suddenly and surprisingly on one figure. An Old Testament commentator on Isaiah, Barry Webb, illustrates

---

13 Graham Cole, *The God who became Human*, (IVP, 2013), 82,83

this convergence of trajectories to his experience of visiting St Peter's Basilica in Rome with his two daughters. He writes:

> At first it was the basilica that captivated us. The whole forecourt seemed designed to produce precisely this effect; the magnificent curving colonnade, the fountain, the grand stair-case, all draw us towards it. But then we noticed the barricades, the seats, the music and the children's choir and realized that quite a deliberate strategy was being put in place to focus our attention elsewhere, at least temporarily. The crowds seemed to be aware of it too, for they were obediently falling into line, so to speak, and expectantly looking across the square towards a far less impressive building situated to the right of the basilica and partly hidden behind a wall. It had long rows of identical windows, so there was no obvious point of interest until about ten minutes to eleven, when a figure appeared briefly at one of the windows and draped a richly coloured banner from it. The effect was immediate. A murmur of anticipation went through the crowd, the volume of music lifted as the choir went into its carefully rehearsed routine, and the basilica receded entirely from our consciousness as every eye became riveted on that one small window. We were soon rewarded. At exactly eleven O' Clock the Pope appeared at the window and addressed us. … At the heart of Isaiah's vision is the startling revelation that the Messiah must suffer. Its sharpest focus is on the one who came to the window for us all.[14]

Another member of the prophetic school of Isaiah looked forward to the coming of the kingdom of God in the future, the time when they will not have to rely on all too human rulers, but God himself will come to rule his people and his world. It will be a time that finally tackles the evils of the world effectively and brings wholeness (*shalom*).

> The wolf shall live with the lamb, the leopard shall lie down with the kid, the calf and the lion and the fatling together, and a little child shall lead them. … The nursing child shall play over the hole of the asp. They will not hurt or destroy on all my holy mountain; for the earth will be full of the knowledge of the Lord as the waters cover the sea (11:6-9).

---

14 Barry Webb, *The Message of Isaiah*, (IVP, 1996), 28

This *shalom* is not merely the absence of hostility. Although Woody Allen may have had a point in suggesting that the lamb will probably have a tough time with the wolf, the overall picture is one of harmony. It is the enjoyment of right relationships with God, others and nature. Professor Bauckham gives a canonical perspective to this passage and develops its ecological significance. He says:

> Peace between people; peace in and with the world of animals. This is a kind of messianic ecology, a return to paradise, a frankly impossible world in which wild animals have changed their diets and their nature. The peace is not merely between predators and prey, but, more specifically, between wild animals and domesticated animals; wolf and lamb, lion and calf, bear and cow. Strikingly, the only humans who appear are children; the little boy leads the lion and the calf as though they were both domestic animals, and the babies play safely around the home of snakes. The reason is surely the innocence and harmlessness of children. In this ideal world from which violence has been banished, those who are always the most unequivocally innocent victims of violence, the children, are finally safe.[15]

We must not take Isaiah's picture literally but we must take it seriously as pointing the way to God's final purpose - the arrival of peace on the basis of the restoration of right relationships.

The Northern Kingdom was never stable and eventually the capital Samaria fell to the Assyrians, a superpower based in what is now Iraq. The Southern Kingdom Judah survived for just over a further century. In 587 BCE it fell to the armies of the Babylonians under King Nebuchadnezzar. For half a century the leaders and the cream of the population lived in exile in Babylon. God seemed to have abandoned his people. An anonymous writer, perhaps a Temple singer, laments the condition to which the remaining population of Judah had been reduced:

---

15 From the Macbride Sermon on the Application of Messianic Prophecy delivered on 26th January 2003, at Hertford College.

How lonely sits the city
that once was full of people!
How like a widow she has become,
she that was great among the nations!
She that was princess among the provinces
has become a vassal (Lamentations 1.1).

Over against this mood of pessimism, the prophets, Isaiah, Jeremiah and Ezekiel pastorally cared for the exiles and kept up their hope for their eventual return to Palestine. In 539 BCE the Persian King, Cyrus conquered the Babylonian Empire and allowed the Jews in exile who wished to return to their homeland to do so. They rebuilt the Temple, the symbol of God's presence in their midst. The prophets glimpse the possibility of a new and better David, the ideal David, a human king so perfectly after God's own heart that his rule would indeed be God's own rule. He would be sent to usher in a kingdom of peace and justice and to fulfil God's eternal covenant with David.

The God of Israel is a promise-keeping God. As Isaiah reminded the despondent Babylonian exiles: 'The grass withers, the flower fades; but the word of our God will stand for ever' (Isaiah 40.8). The narrative shape of the three 'flight passages' of these foundational promises involves a movement from the *particular* to the *universal*: the *blessing promised to Abraham* is to overflow to all people; the *revelation of God's power and glory shown through the nation Israel* is to be made known to all the nations; and the *reign of King David from Zion* anticipates the universal realization of God's kingdom in all creation.

Such a holistic mission cannot be the responsibility of any one individual. That is surely why God dreamed up the idea of the church. The ringing slogan of the Lausanne movement points to the connection between ecclesiology and missiology when it speaks of 'the whole church taking the whole gospel to the whole world'. Such a holistic mission has a whole-creation and whole-humanity perspective. It consists of the proclamation of the gospel and social concern about issues of justice and ecology. As a 'catholic' community the church must constantly reach beyond itself to those from 'every tribe and tongue and people and nation' (Revelation. 5.9). Rowan Williams puts it succinctly when he says: 'the church is a community whose only interest is the interest of all'.

Now: From everywhere to everywhere

The mission of the Church today is to join in the sending flow laid out in the three trajectories we have considered in the Old Testament back-story. It is setting off from the *particular* and following the Biblical direction towards the *universal*. But whereas the three trajectories we have considered had a geographical nuance, moving for instance, from Jerusalem to the ends of the earth, mission in the globalized world of today, is a movement of God's people from 'everywhere to everywhere'.[16] Travel and immigration coupled with the internet have made it nearly impossible for Christianity or any other 'world view' to have complete supremacy. Mission is no longer tied to any particular geographical direction. The command of the Great Commission to make disciples of 'all the nations' (Matthew 28.19) applies not only to 'all geographical locations of people' but to 'all sections of society'. As Bauckham points out, 'this new centre is everywhere and nowhere, just as with the advent of modern geography and postmodern globalization the ends of the earth are now everywhere and nowhere'.[17]

Christians cannot embrace pluralism as an end in itself but they do need to come to terms with the fact that plurality of viewpoints is here to stay and think creatively and positively about how to evangelize without sucking up too much to the culture. Sometimes Christians have adopted an adversarial approach to secular society and turned churches into little political bases. This has resulted in poisoning many people's view of the church as only being interested in power. Others withdraw from engaging in the world outside the church, seeing nothing good in it.

---

16 Richard Bauckham borrows this phrase from the title of the book by Michael Nazir-Ali, *From Everywhere to Everywhere*, (Collins, London, 1991)
17 Richard Bauckham, *Bible and Mission: Christian Witness in a Postmodern World*, (Baker Academic, 2003), 76

Sometimes, the geographical thrust of mission will be *centripetal*, attracting people through witness and compassionate action into the church community. At other times, the geographical direction of the mission will be *centrifugal*, as God's people go out from the church community and engage with their neighbourhoods. Both directions of mission are evident in the Old and the New Testaments. They are not mutually exclusive. The *centripetal* focus is perhaps most evident in the Fourth Gospel when Jesus says, 'I, when I am lifted up from the earth, will draw all people to myself' (John 12.32). The *centrifugal* focus sets the agenda for mission in the book of Acts: 'But you will receive power when the Holy Spirit has come upon you; and you will be my witnesses in Jerusalem, in all Judea and Samaria, and to the ends of the earth' (Acts 1.8).

In aspiring to be faithful to this *universal* goal we must be aware of the postmodern criticism of grand meta-narratives as being projects of power and domination, a kind of narrative imperialism or ecclesiastical globalization. Against this, it is important to keep in mind that, far from being oppressive, the people of God in the Old Testament were themselves subjected to one Super-power after another: the Egyptians, the Assyrians, the Babylonians, the Persians, the Greeks and the Romans. More than that, as Graham Cole has remarked:

> This cosmic narrative has at its heart not a pantocrator's tyranny or benevolent dictatorship but the brutal death of a victim. There can be no universal statements without at the same time focusing on someone bleeding and suffocating on a cross. Paradoxically, this victim is the cosmic ruler; his rule is achieved through the experience of suffering, and his peace-making is accomplished through the absorption of violence.[18]

The biblical story is not one of human mastery and the mission of the church to universalize the gospel story should never mean foisting it upon others by repressing human freedom and diversity. Christian witness must always be non-coercive. The *universal* that is the Kingdom of

---

18 Graham A. Cole, *God the Peacemaker*, (IVP, 2009), 256

God is no dreary uniformity or oppressive denial of difference. Within this movement-mission into the new future of God, Ben Myers poses a couple of significant questions for our Church to ponder as we engage in our ferocious and dishonouring debates over same-sex marriage and the place of lesbian, gay, bisexual, transgender and intersex people in the ministry of the church. He says:

> In terms of inclusiveness and equality, for Paul, "Jew" and "Gentile" are now obsolete ethnic/religious categories. And the same goes for the social category of slave and free, and the gender category of male and female: all are one in Christ (Galatians 3:28). And following the trajectory, we might ask a radical contemporary question: How big is your "all"? Is your "all" perhaps too small?[19]

These questions also have application to the ecumenical movement. I cannot find denominational differences in the description of the 'new heaven and new earth' in Revelation 21. If they are not there, how can they be here? In the new creation, the tribes will join together with others from every people, language and nation to praise the One who sits on the throne.

Bauckham qualifies the three mission trajectories we have considered with a vitally important fourth trajectory that reaches *all* only by way of the *least*.[20] But even with this qualification, there remains in our pluralistic culture an unavoidable *scandal of particularity*. St Peter expresses this in his preaching when he focuses the biblical story on the person and work of Christ and proclaims: 'There is salvation in no one else, for there is no other name under heaven given among mortals by which we must ("of necessity", *"dei"*) be saved' (Acts 4.12). We must redouble our efforts, abounding in love, to make known the Christ who saves all who come to God by him. Whenever this happens, we will rejoice. At the same time, we must remember that this is the Spirit's work and not ours and repudiate any attempt to coerce or manipulate people

---

19 See www.faith-theology.com/ 'What is the opposite of faith?' posted by Kim Fabricius, Monday, 29 June, 2015
20 Bauckham, op.cit., 98

into conversion. Indeed, although the evangelistic task confronting the church is enormous, it is probably a good thing for some of us to shut up and sit down occasionally! Witnessing to our faith in Jesus must never be anxiety-driven or a frantic assertion of ourselves.

When we meet with those with whom we disagree, our initial approach should be to listen and then to attempt to expand the conversation so that our own understanding might increase. Better to be intrigued than threatened by difference. This is not to say that dialogue entails the compromise of fundamental beliefs or that the issue of truth is a matter of indifference. But there is a proper kind of humility which, even as we proclaim our conviction of truth, obliges us to acknowledge with respect the richness of another's devotion to what they have received as truth. None of us has received the whole truth as God knows it. We all have things to learn.

Questions for reflection

1. The old cliché about 'not mentioning religion, sex, and politics in polite company is very much a reality of modernity'. How can Christians be helped to witness to their faith?

2. Post-modernists pose the question: 'is not the church's attempt to evangelize the world by universalizing the biblical story, nothing more than an oppressive power play?' In the light of this chapter, how would you respond to this question?

3. The statement 'all roads lead to God' is ignorant, naïve and patronizing because the major religions are fundamentally different from each other. Some believe in one God (Islam, Judaism), some in a more complicated three-in-one God (Christianity), some in many gods (Hinduism), some in no God at all (some types of Buddhism). Each of these five major religions makes uncompromising claims to be true. How can we build trust with other faith groups as we celebrate Jesus as the way, the truth and the life for us and for all people?

Prayer:

Lord, you know us and yet call us, imperfect though we are, to bring your blessing, your light and your kingdom to this world. You know us, and yet you call us to be vessels of your grace. That you should trust us with this mission is too difficult to grasp, and the task, in our own strength is impossible. You know us and call us, but more importantly, by your Spirit we implore you to empower us. We make our prayer through Christ our Lord. Amen

4. The Story of the Messiah

The incarnation

Jesus is the epicentre and climax of the storyline of Israel, the one in whom God made God-self known most spectacularly and most fully. He is the visible image of the invisible God, the one in whom 'the whole fullness of deity dwells bodily' (Colossians 2.8). As we read the Gospels, we need to remind ourselves that we are living in a situation that generation upon generation before Jesus could only dream about. For them, even God's name remained unspoken; that's how distant humanity felt they were from God. Then God chose to come and live among us. The remote God was found to be near in Jesus.

An elderly parishioner shared with me something that had been niggling at him over many years about his Christian faith. He explained that throughout his life he had no difficulty in believing the teaching of Jesus, but he wanted to know: 'who was running the show while he was down here?' Like that man, there are many who feel perplexed by the scandalous thought of God coming to this earth as the male-embodied Jesus, the fullness of God in the embryo. Who would have been persuaded by gazing upon the tiny mite lying in a manger that they were in the presence of the creator God? In our frustration we too might admit that we don't 'get it' and puzzle over the same question that was put to me by my elderly friend - 'who was running the show while he was down here?'

Whatever we may imagine about the spiritual rhapsody that attended the angelic announcement made by the angel Gabriel to Mary, its accomplishment was something that took place in the physical realm – the realm of gynaecology and obstetrics. Mary would soon be nurturing Jesus in her womb and that in turn meant that God would be dependent on her. The Most High God would entrust himself to her body and share the risk of a first century pregnancy. There was no fancy birthing suite. No midwife would be present in the stable. There would certainly be no epidural available. Moreover, the incarnation is not confined to the birth in a stable. Incarnation happens in Bethlehem and Nazareth and Jerusalem and along the dusty roads between them.

The mystery put to me by my devout and elderly parishioner was not one that I could 'crack open' for him. The incarnation cannot easily be crystallized into a verbal formula. The Council of Chalcedon's definition of AD 451 on Christ's person in two natures may be sound orthodoxy but it can easily come across as an attempt to avoid the reality of Jesus' presence and to avoid mediating that presence. It is essential to remember that our creeds are a kind of conceptual map. They mark out and safeguard the mysterious, twofold identity of Jesus Christ with the divine and human natures united in his identity 'without confusion, change, separation, or division'.[1] As the divine Son of God he was not a hybrid between humanity and divinity that is neither one nor the other. To try and stress one nature of the Son more than the other will always end up in problems. Jesus is the Word who became flesh, he is God with us. He is not God and man (some sort of two Son Christology), but God who became a particular man whose flesh was bloodied from his circumcision on the eighth day. We can't shelve 'bits' of him in order to talk about other 'bits'. We can't part-him or divide him from himself.

In the final analysis, the job of the more abstract style Christology is to hold us still before the divine mystery in reverence and awe. Our resources to speak about it are sparse. Our language is deplorably clumsy. At the end of our conversation I referred my aged friend and parishioner to some words of John Henry Newman when he said, 'ten thousand difficulties do not make one doubt'. Many people worry about doubting their faith if they are puzzled by their beliefs. But there is a difference between doubt and difficulty. The difference has been explained in this way. The person with a difficulty says, *'How can this be so?'* whereas a person who doubts says, *'That can't be so'.* The first statement expresses difficulty, but a willingness to believe. The second statement expresses doubt and unwillingness to believe.

1 Part of the classic definition at the Council of Chalcedon in 451

The person with difficulties says, *'Lord, I believe: help my unbelief'.*
The person with doubt says, *'I don't believe Lord, and don't bother to
help my unbelief'.* I tried to reassure my questioning friend that there is
more ultimate faith in the person who, like himself, desires to come to
a better understanding than in the person who glibly recites the creed
each Sunday but has never seriously faced the difficulties. At least he
can understand and sympathize with those who struggle with issues of
faith and hopefully, by continuing to love the Lord with all the grey
matter he has been given, emerge stronger in his faith.

The staggering claim at the heart of the incarnation – God scaling
Godself down to the dimensions of God the child - involved risk-taking
humility. St Paul pondered the 'bowing-down' of God to the level of
each and every person when he recorded the beautiful words of a hymn
in his letter to the Philippians:

> Jesus' state was divine,
> yet he did not cling
> to his equality with God
> but emptied himself
> to assume the condition of a slave,
> and became as we are;
> and, being as we all are,
> he was humbler yet,
> even to accepting death,
> death on a cross[2] (Philippians 2.6-8).

God's love was revealed in the mystery and the extravagance of the
divinity *'pouring itself out'* to become a helpless baby relying for
everything on his mother. God had chosen to hang on a mother's breast
in total dependency. In submitting to the process of conception and
birth, God reveals the extent to which he will go out of love for the
world. And the cross, as we shall see, was the culmination of the same
process. Paradoxically, however, the self-emptying of the incarnation
did not imply, as my friend appeared to think, an equation that amounts
to saying: incarnation = God minus. On the contrary, the biblical

2 From the Jerusalem Bible, using inclusive language.

equation is: incarnation = God plus. In terms of the classical Athanasian Creed (sixth century), the incarnation is 'not the conversion of Godhead into flesh' but 'the assumption of manhood into God'.

We so easily forget that Christianity is a material religion. It concerns an historical incarnation, a flesh and blood crucifixion, a bodily resurrection, and it culminates in the taking up of our full humanity into the Godhead which we call the ascension. The ascension marks the final destiny of humanity. It provides the template or pattern of what God ultimately intends to do with us and for us. The material bread and wine of the Eucharist reinforce this principle. The consecrated elements become for us the spiritual means of grace through which we encounter the living Lord. Rowan Williams explains that this is why they are accorded reverence:

> It is why the Book of Common Prayer tells you that you need to consume reverently at the end of Holy Communion what is left over. Here is something of the world that has been identified as carrying the power and love of God to you. Don't just throw it away. Make what you will of this tradition of reverence for the consecrated things; but it does at least suggest that to take seriously the material food of bread and wine can be the beginning of a proper and grateful reverence before all God's material things – a doorway into seeing all things as demanding reverent attention, even contemplation.[3]

Professor Daniel Kirk has attempted to draw out the implications of the incarnation for contemporary believers with another set of equations. He argues that Jesus' humanity has too often been seen only in terms of his suitability to be a fitting sacrifice by leading a sinless life. He claims that people seem to draw the following mental equation in regard to the two natures of Christ: 'God'='awesome' and 'man'='suck'. He expands this equation by saying:

> Jesus is human. This is because (a) we suck, so (b) Jesus has to be able to die for us.

---

3 Rowan Williams, *Being Christian*, (SPCK, 2014), 50,51

The only value to be found in his humanity was his death. Or, if we wanted to expand it a little bit, as in Hebrews, we might say that he occupied the same sucky existence we have (temptations to sin and the like) but managed to get to the cross unscathed.

So he could die for us. Because we suck![4]

The implication seems to be that to describe Jesus as 'sinless' in a culture which has largely rejected the whole notion of sin, may imply that he was part of the nerdy team instead of being the radical, life-loving, unshockable Jesus that the Gospel's portray. In her daring speculations, Sheila Cassidy spells out what this 'suckiness' might mean in terms with which many of us can more easily identify. She says:

Perhaps, like us, he was unwittingly hurtful, even picked his nose when no-one was looking. He had friends, men friends and women too, some close, perhaps very close. Was he celibate? We assume so. Did he yearn sometimes for sexual intimacy? Surely, for he was a normal man, flesh of our flesh. Why, I wonder, do we shy away from even thinking of Jesus in this way? When, from time to time, film directors have the courage to portray Jesus in modern guise with normal emotions and sexual fantasies, we blush and look away or get hurt and angry and talk of blasphemy. But surely this is nonsense. Why do we need a pale sexless softly-spoken Jesus with soulful brown eyes any more than we need a sugar-coated, luminous, blue-eyed virgin to be the mother of our God.[5]

Whereas the Pharisees of his day maintained their holiness by picking up their skirts and running like mad from whatever and whoever was considered unclean, Jesus reached out and touched (or allowed himself to be touched) by the very ones who were unclean! A song from the Iona Community, 'The Touching Place' brings together the touch of Christ and the touch of his followers:

4 See http://www.jrdkirk.com/2015/05/19/why-is-jesus-human/ and forthcoming book, J.R.Daniel Kirk, *A Man Attested by God: the Human Jesus of the Synoptic Gospels.*
5 Sheila Cassidy, *Good Friday People*, (DLT, 1991), 10

To the lost Christ shows his face
To the unloved he gives his embrace;
To those who cry in pain or disgrace,
Christ makes with his friends a touching place.[6]

Jesus holiness flowed in the reverse direction to the holiness of the Pharisees. Instead of being contaminated by those regarded as unclean, he overcame uncleanness by spreading wholeness. Mark Achtemeier makes the point with arresting force. He says:

> Jesus' holiness is an active power that crashes the barriers between pure and impure. Jesus' holiness enters in love and mercy into all the dark precincts of ungodliness and abomination, and there plants seeds of healing.[7]

Such a positive, dynamic understanding challenges our tendencies towards the holiness of the Pharisees that leads us to want to separate ourselves from those we consider too 'unclean' or 'other,' whatever 'unclean' or 'other' may mean for us. Friendship itself is often eclipsed today by the tendency to see 'others' only in terms of usefulness and productivity. Wesley Hill cites the challenging words of a sermon by John Henry Newman in which he makes the following comments about Jesus particular friendship with one of his disciples (John 13.23; 19.26; 20.2; 21.7,20).

> Much might be said on this remarkable circumstance. I say *remarkable*, because it might be supposed that the Son of God Most High could not have loved one man more than another; or again, if so, that He would not have had only one friend, but, as being All-holy, He would have loved all men more or less, in proportion to their holiness. Yet we find our Saviour had a private friend; and this shows us, first, how entirely He was a man, as much as any of us, in His wants and feelings.[8]

---

6 Hymn 677 in *Together in Song: Australian Hymn Book 11*, (HarperCollins, 1999)
7 Mark Achtemeier, *'The Holiness of Christ,'* in an address to the National Celebration of Confessing Churches, Atlanta Georgia, February 26, 2002
8 In Wesley Hill, *Spiritual Friendship: Finding Love in the Church as a Celibate Gay Christian*, (Brazos Press, 2015) 53

It is clear from the letter to the Hebrews that the 'perfection' of Christ is not a static 'perfection'. According to this writer, he had to go through a process of suffering in order to be made 'perfect'.

> Although he was a Son, he learned obedience through what he suffered; and having been made perfect, he became the source of eternal salvation for all who obey him (Hebrews 5.8,9).

Following the great twentieth century theologian, Karl Barth, I take the view that the writer of Hebrews is implying that in the incarnation, Christ assumed *fallen* human flesh, but by the Spirit was enabled to overcome the temptations and inclinations of that flesh and to offer himself as a perfect obedient sacrifice for sin. Such a dynamic view of 'perfection' seems to me to be much more wonderful than the alternative view that in the incarnation Christ was given as it were a 'clean slate', standing where Adam was before the 'Fall' rather than where Adam was after the 'Fall'. However, I am also conscious of the fact that the discomfort that many feel in speaking of Jesus humanity in terms of being 'without sin' may be driven more by the Western World's rejection of both the sinfulness of human nature and the consequent need for Jesus' sacrificial death on the cross. But I am jumping ahead of myself.

What has always been clear to Christians from the earliest times is that the Bible presents Jesus as the living embodiment of the loving Lord, 'truly and fully divine' and 'absolutely and thoroughly human' or in theological-speak, both *homoousion* with God and *homoousion* with us[9]. In Professor Tom Torrance's words, 'God has the transcendent freedom to go outside God-self to become what he is not, without ceasing to be what he eternally is'.[10] This language fits with the evidence of the Gospels but it doesn't explain the metaphysical conundrum. It merely takes us to the limits of our human grasp. From that point, as we saw earlier, we must allow the poets and hymn writers to help us to marvel

---

9 *Homoousion*, the term used in the Nicene Creed to express the relations of the Father and the Son within the Godhead. It means 'of the same substance'.
10 T. F. Torrance, *Theology in Reconciliation*, (Geoffrey Chapman, 1975), 224

at the mystery. Henry R Bramley's hymn, *The great God of heaven is come down to earth,* causes my soul to soar with this verse:

> The word in the bliss of the Godhead remains,
> Yet in flesh comes to suffer the keenest of pains;
> He is that He was, and forever shall be,
> But becomes what He was not, for you and for me.[11]

Among other things, this mystery says something to all of us about the profound value of human beings. There is so much in our society and world in general that gives the message to whole groups, classes and nations, 'You are not worth attending to'. Who 'bows down' to the homeless addict? If God divests God-self of divine majesty and becomes subject to all the physical and physiological awarenesses that make up distinctively human experience, then surely human life is worth living and people are worth serving and saving. It is this conviction that fired the anger of people all around the world at Indonesia's cruel and inhumane action in executing by firing squad the two Australian drug traffickers, Andrew Chan and Myuran Sukumaran and five of their own people on the 28th April, 2015. At the time of writing, the world is facing an unprecedented humanitarian crisis with 60 million desperate displaced people fleeing persecution and life threatening conflicts. The heart-wrenching images of three-year-old Syrian toddler, Aylan Kurdi, whose lifeless body was washed up on the shore of Turkey, after a failed boat crossing to Greece, is a challenge to Governments across the world to face up to our common responsibility and our common humanity. In God's kingdom, no one is superfluous. There are no waste people. God's love enacted in Jesus's particular history holds aloof from no one. We who live in the Western World live in an 'upwardly mobile' culture. By contrast, as Brian McLaren has put it, in the person of Jesus, God is seen to be:

> 'downwardly mobile' – down into Mary's womb, down into a stable, down into the mess of human injustice and need.[12]

---

11 Last verse of original hymn as printed in the old English Hymnal. (NEH 37)
12 Brian McLaren, *Naked Spirituality*, (HarperOne, 2011), 208

Or, as Rowan Williams compellingly remarked:

> The love of God is a love that goes where God is not supposed to be, where God is not imagined or conceived to be. ... God's love is recognizable precisely as that love which goes where it has no business to go and which lives, blossoms and acts in the place of the curse, in the place where God is forgotten.[13]

Jesus reshaped what it means to belong to the people of God. He was nicknamed 'a friend of whores'. To be with him, is to be with the 'non-belongers'. As the edgy South African Archbishop, Desmond Tutu, remarks: 'we may be surprised at the people we find in heaven. God has a soft spot for sinners. His standards are quite low'.[14]

The miracles

Dr Barry Marshall a former chaplain at Trinity College, Melbourne had a brilliant mind and a cheeky sense of humour. On one occasion he offered the following advice to a group of young men about to be ordained to the priesthood:

> Always comfort kindly, preach intelligently, but never, never, mystify. Cut out the supernatural stuff, all that intersects the world of flesh and blood. You will be very popular and when you retire, you will be given a fine, marble clock on which to number the rest of your useless days more accurately![15]

Dr Marshall knew that after their ordination, his students would be ministering in a culture where scientific scepticism holds sway and the divide between 'natural' and 'supernatural' would be a major stumbling block to faith. He recognised that the Biblical writers make no distinction between 'secular' and 'sacred' or 'natural' and 'supernatural'. The person of faith can discern God's marvellous activity at work in both the regular and the random events of creation. In fact, the Bible writers

---

13 Rowan Williams, *'The Surprising Love of God'*, a sermon at Fairacres for the Feast of the Holy Cross, 14th September, 2006
14 Tutu, *'Desmond Tutu Peace Foundation.'* Accessed December 4, 2012. http://www. tutufoundation-usa-org/exhibitions.html.
15 From an article in the Ridley College Magazine in the 1960's.

never use the word 'miracle' or 'supernatural.' They make no distinction in the causality of events. For them, nothing is 'natural' in the sense that it happens by itself. God is involved and active in everything – in the routine events as well as the remarkable events. God is involved with and cares for the life and death of every single sparrow.

For the Biblical authors, what we call a 'miracle' is a way of referring to one of the ways God acts. God was involved in the conception of Jesus without a human father but God is also involved in forming a child in the womb as the result of sexual intercourse between a man and a woman. God opens and closes the womb. When we speak of God 'miraculously intervening' we are assuming the post-enlightenment division between the 'natural' and 'supernatural' spheres which was unknown in Biblical times. For them there was no 'natural' sphere. They didn't confine God's activity to the inexplicable gaps in their knowledge. They believed that God is active in an interior way, at every level all the time, working with both 'law' and 'chance' for his own good purpose.

In his sermon on the day of Pentecost, the apostle Peter employed three words to describe Jesus' remarkable acts. He referred to them as:

> *deeds of power*, *wonders* and *signs* that God did through him (Jesus) among you (Acts 2.22).

In these three descriptors, Peter points to the *origin, effect* and *character* of the so-called miracles.

1. 'Deeds of power' points to their origin.

The so-called miracles are expressions of the sovereign power of God. In his home town of Nazareth, the astonished locals exclaimed:

> Where did this man get all this? What is this wisdom that has been given to him? What deeds of power are being done by his hands! (Mark 6:2)

The crowds were perplexed as to the origin of Jesus' mighty deeds and his authoritative words. In his Gospel, Mark strategically seeks to show that Jesus is in some way to be identified with the one God of Israel. The miracle of Jesus calming the sea in Mark 4:35-41, is a passage strongly reminiscent of Psalm 107:23-29, where sailors cry out to God and the storm is calmed:

> Some went down to the sea in ships, doing business on the mighty waters; they saw the deeds of the Lord, his wondrous works in the deep. For he commanded and raised the stormy wind, which lifted up the waves of the sea. They mounted up to heaven, they went down to the depths; their courage melted away in their calamity; they reeled and staggered like drunkards, and were at their wits' end. Then they cried to the Lord in their trouble, and he brought them out from their distress; he made the storm be still, and the waves and the sea were hushed.

Mark superimposes the account of Jesus stilling the storm on to the background of the Psalm 107. For Mark, the unanswered question that the disciples ask each other in awe, 'Who is this, that even the wind and sea obey him?' can only have one answer, but true to form, Mark leaves it as an open question. As we read the story of the stilling of the storm through Mark's eyes we are drawn into the contemplation of a paradoxical revelation that shatters our categories and exceeds our understanding. We can only get at the overwhelming truth of who Jesus really is through hints and allusions that project the story of Jesus onto the background of Israel's story.

The stilling of the storm points to a much deeper presence of God in Jesus than popular political ideas circulating in the community about the Messiah. Mark seeks to guard against the way labels and 'truth statements' can corrupt truths that are impossible to fully articulate.

But whereas Mark is circumspect in communicating the mystery of Jesus' identity and the source of his powerful deeds, the author of the fourth Gospel leaves the reader in no doubt that these deeds of power were not Jesus' own, 'done by his own hands'. They were the Father's work, though they were granted to the Son for him to accomplish:

> The works that the Father has given me to complete, the very works that I am doing, testify on my behalf that the Father has sent me (John 5:36).

In their own distinctive ways, both Mark and John understood that the *'deeds of power'* originated with God.

2. 'Wonders' points to their effect

Again and again, people were utterly astounded both at the authority of Jesus' teaching and his miraculous powers. After the healing of a paralytic man Mark says:

> They were all amazed and glorified God, saying, "We have never seen anything like this!" (Mark 2:12).

The first-century Jewish writer, Josephus, describes Jesus as 'one who performed amazing feats'. The expression 'amazing or surprising feats' translates the Greek *'paradoxa erga'*, literally *'baffling deeds'*.

Yet, these *'baffling deeds'* of Jesus were not merely displays of power or conjuring tricks to make people stand and stare. Indeed, those who see Jesus as a purveyor of power failed to understand him. Mark's Gospel makes it clear that he can be rightly understood only as the Son of Man who will surrender power in order to suffer and die. It was for this reason that sometimes Jesus declined a request to perform a miracle and at other times commanded a person to tell no one about it. Both the refusal to give a sign and the command to silence, were because of the popular misunderstanding that saw Jesus' purely as a stunning wonder worker.

The *'wonders'* of Jesus were not revelations of an unreasonable, arbitrary figure who was content to show himself here and not there so that people missed out on knowing him if they were in the wrong place at the wrong time. The Gospels tell us that the effect of these *'wonders'* on the person with a 'seeing eye' and 'understanding heart' was not simply astonishment. It was faith. Humble people saw. They understood and they believed.

3. 'Signs' points to their character

The so-called Apocryphal Gospels make much of the inexplicable deeds that Jesus performed but they come across as being childish exhibitions of power. For instance, in one of these Gospels, the boy Jesus is said to have made clay models of birds and then clapped his hands and the birds rose and flew away. Such stunning occurrences are clever but they serve no purpose. They may have been 'deeds of power'. But they served no spiritual or moral purpose.

By contrast, Jesus' deeds of immediacy are described no less than seventeen times by the Fourth Evangelist as *'signs'*. The background to his use of the term lies with the Old Testament prophets, such as Isaiah who stripped naked and walked around Jerusalem as a sign of judgment against Egypt. So too the essence of a *sign* for John was that it was a symbol-laden act, rich in meaning for those with eyes to see.

Moreover, for John, it was always a public act done by Jesus not merely before his disciples but before an unbelieving world. The changing of water into wine; the feeding of the multitude and the various healings including the resuscitation of Lazarus from the dead all share in common that they have as their audience people other than Jesus' followers. By contrast, Jesus' walking on the water, is not part of Jesus' public ministry but occurs privately before the disciples, and so is not referred to by the author of John as one of the seven signs that Jesus performed.

Each of John's seven *'signs'* were like *sign-posts* pointing to God's glory displayed in Jesus and so revealing Jesus as God's true representative. In effect, they were like parables, told not in words but in deeds, and conveyed an inner hidden meaning.

After the changing of the water into wine at the wedding in Cana, John says:

> Jesus did this, the first of his signs, in Cana of Galilee, and revealed his glory; and his disciples believed in him (John 2:11).

To sum up the New Testament teaching, we can say that the *'mighty deeds'* of immediacy accomplished by Jesus originated in God's sovereign power. As *'wonders'* their effect was to produce awe and astonishment but they were not arbitrary, meaningless displays of power. For people of faith, they had the character of *'signs'* pointing to the glory of God and to Jesus' true identity as the Son of God and the inauguration of the Kingdom of God. That is to say, they were significant.

Where does all this leave us today? It is important to understand the origin, effect and character of the apparently random deeds that Jesus performed in the first century, but is he still at work in this way in the 21st century?

Ultimately, everyone negotiates this kind of question in terms of their notion of God. Those who reject miracles because they believe the universe to be a closed system, do not see the anomaly of dictating to the Creator what he is permitted to do in his own creation. God is not trapped in the creation. God is sovereign. The dogmatic rejection of *mighty deeds, marvellous manifestations* or *transparent moments* in Jesus' ministry has little to do with evidence and a lot to do with existing assumptions about what is possible in the universe.

Can we then, draw a straight line from the pages of the New Testament to our situation today, say, in regard, to the healing ministry of Jesus? Well, yes, I think we can draw a line but I suggest that it is a somewhat staggered line rather than a straight line. It has sometimes been claimed that there are probably more miracles than many mainline Christians are open to seeing but far fewer than many Pentecostal and Charismatic Christians claim on the flimsiest of evidence. As mentioned above, it would be bizarre to put the Creator in a straitjacket and declare that miracles can't and don't happen. But on the other hand, we have no liberty to say (as some do) that performing miracles is the normal Christian life. John Stott has said, 'I am convinced that miracles cannot be described as "normal". Indeed, any definition of miracles must include the fact that they are abnormal, and are deviations from God's normal mode of working'.[16]

Christian healing is a messy mystery. It often raises agonizing questions and yields results that are very hard to categorise. In Biblical terms, all healing is divine healing. God has put in the human body remarkable

16 David L. Edwards with John Stott, *Essentials*, (Hodder & Stoughton, 1988), 216

therapeutic and recuperative powers. Charismatic and Pentecostal Christians have sometimes been inclined to discern God's activity only in miraculous happenings, which turns God into some kind of magician and overlooks God's activity in the normalities and regularities which scientists call 'natural laws'.

In pastoral terms, in praying for healing, we must make it clear that we are not trying dictate to God or manipulate God by claiming something that God has not promised, such as is done by those who claim that God always heals. Period! In our prayers, we can only plead with God, as Paul did in praying for a 'thorn in the flesh' to be taken away (2 Corinthians 12.7,8). Alas! The 'thorn' (whatever it was) remained. Like Paul, we can only plead for healing because physical healing in this life lies in God's sovereign good pleasure. We must not presume upon God when present physical healing is not something that God has promised. God's saving work is not yet done. We are caught up in an interim period between what is and what shall be. Graham Cole urges us to adopt a biblical realism when he writes:

> The tension between 'the now and the not yet' will be relieved by the resurrection of the body, and by the establishment of the new heavens and the new earth. The final answer to the healing question will be the glorified body of which Paul writes'.[17]

But that day is not yet and as John Stott soberly warned, 'we cannot tamper with God's clock' nor 'attempt to gate-crash heaven'.[18]

Other Christians have little or no expectation that God will act in response to prayer. Colin Buchanan is surely right when he urges Christians to be more expectant. He says:

> Worship is not and will not be the sum of the various parts we have planned. God has more for us, and we have more for Him, than we anticipated whilst planning.[19]

---

17 Graham Cole, *God the Peacemaker*, 2009, IVP, 245
18 John Stott, *Focus on Christ*, 1979, Collins Fount, 89 & 91
19 Colin Buchanan, *Encountering Charismatic Worship*, Grove Booklet 51, 23

We must allow the Spirit to work a 'revolution of rising expectation' as we gather for worship. In effect, as we intercede for another we are saying something like this: 'Here you are in all your very great need and here is God in all his great power. What we are going to do now as we lay our hands upon you and hold you in prayer, is to bring these two things together and wait to see what God will do. We cannot control the answer but we have good reason to believe that it will always be gracious even when it is not the answer we are looking for'.

The kingdom

Bishop Tom Wright insists that the Gospels are essentially stories which tell how Jesus became King - the anointed one, the Messiah. In other words, they announce the launch of a 'theocracy' when ultimately the kingdom will 'come on earth as it is in heaven'. In the meantime, we live between the kingdom inaugurated and the kingdom consummated. This 'now' and 'not yet' tension can be illustrated by looking at just one chapter in Luke's Gospel. The presence of the kingdom is apparent in Jesus' healing miracles: 'But if it is by the finger of God that I cast out demons, then the kingdom of God has come to you' (Luke 11.20). In the words of John Dickson, 'the kingdom is *here* not merely *near*'.[20] Yet earlier in the same chapter we read that Jesus encouraged his disciples to pray for the consummation of the kingdom - 'Your kingdom come' (Luke 11.2).

One sign of the presence of the kingdom is the gift of God's Holy Spirit who enables the fruit of 'love, joy, peace, patience, kindness, generosity, faithfulness, gentleness and self-control' to blossom now in the believer's life (Galatians 5.22,23). Yet the Spirit is but a foretaste of what is in store for us. Paul employs two images to reinforce this tension in the Spirit's role. He speaks of the Spirit as one of the *'first fruits'* given as we wait for our final redemption and as the *'deposit'* guaranteeing our future inheritance (Romans 8.23 and Ephesians 1.14). It is not easy to maintain this tension.

---

20 John Dickson, *A Doubter's Guide To The Bible*, 2014, Zondervan, 146

In addition to this eschatological tension between the 'now' and the 'not yet', Tom Wright has pointed to another tension in our Lord's teaching about the kingdom when he speaks of Jesus as the 'kingdom-bringer' and the 'cross-bearer'. This comes to the fore during a great watershed moment in Jesus' teaching in the pagan district of Caesarea Philippi. Jesus led up to it by asking what people were saying about him, and who they took him to be. Some said he was John the Baptist, the forerunner of the Messiah. But John the Baptist had several times asserted that he was not the Messiah. Others said he was Elijah; and still others, that he was one of the great prophets (Mark 8.27-35). To this day the Jews leave a chair vacant for Elijah when they celebrate the Passover, because the prophet Malachi had taught that when Elijah comes, the Messiah will not be very far away (Malachi 4.5). Having heard the verdicts of the crowd, Jesus asks the disciples themselves the all-important question: 'but who do you say that I am?' Simon Peter responds with his great confession: 'You are the Messiah!' (Mark 8:29). Immediately Jesus goes on to predict his own suffering and crucifixion by a political coalition of Israel and Rome. Peter refused to accept such a possibility and strongly protests. He was determined to have nothing to do with a 'crucified kingdom-bringer' because he was still thinking in terms of a conquering Messiah, who would sweep the Romans from Palestine and lead Israel to power. It is as though he saw himself as the proto-type of the modern freedom-fighter whose rallying cry was - 'throw a grenade for Jesus'! But the Palm Sunday procession when Jesus rode into Jerusalem on the back of a donkey would be a clear contradiction of this political expectation. Jesus riding on a donkey was an acted parable or piece of street drama, in deliberate fulfilment of the words of the Old Testament prophet, Zechariah:

> Tell the daughter of Zion, look, your King is coming to you, humble, and mounted on a donkey, and on a colt, the foal of a donkey (Zechariah 9:9).

This was no revolutionary, violent demonstration of brute force but a demonstration of the Messiah's reign of humility as he enters Jerusalem.

It becomes even more apparent when the Zechariah verse is seen in its original context which makes explicit the contrast between the peace donkey and the war horse. The very next verse in the original prophecy reads :

> He (God) will cut off the chariot from Ephraim and the war horse from Jerusalem; and the battle bow shall be cut off, and he shall command peace to the nations (Zechariah 9:10).

The kingdom's reign does not depend on military manoeuvres, for the simple reason, as Jesus was soon to tell Pilate, his kingdom was not of this world.

At Caesarea Philippi, Jesus had tried to convey to Peter and the other disciples the notion of a 'single kingdom-and-cross reality'. There is a cost involved in being a 'follower' as distinct from a 'fan' of Jesus. In the light of this, Wright goes on to compare different churches today in broad terms as being either 'cross churches' or 'kingdom churches' or to put it another way, churches which stress either 'evangelism' or 'social action'.

In 'cross churches' he claims, the only thing that matters is rescuing the perishing. The atonement is proclaimed as a rescue operation concerned with 'snatching a few souls from the fire'[21]. Social activity is regarded as a waste of time in view of the imminent return of the Lord. There is very little concern about God's kingdom coming. After all, there is little point in hanging new curtains or rearranging the furniture when the house is on fire. For 'cross churches', the only thing that matters, Wright claims, is 'saving souls for a disembodied eternity'.

Another influential critic of so-called 'cross churches' is the American Evangelical activist and editor of Sojourners magazine, Jim Wallis. In critiquing Mel Gibson's film, 'The Passion of Christ', Wallis wrote:

> I never really heard much about the kingdom in my evangelical church; everything was about the atonement. And that's what I fear in Gibson's film. But the passion of Christ makes no sense apart

---

21 N. T. Wright, *Simply Good News*, (HarperOne, 2015), 124

from the kingdom of God.... Where is the central message of Jesus – the coming of a new order called the kingdom of God – which would turn everything about our lives and world upside down? ... (The film) turns the 33 years of the life of Christ into a period of almost wasted time – just getting Jesus ready to be the blood sacrifice. He had to put in time to grow up enough to be killed. ... Where is the whole new way of living he brought to us and told us to follow in a new community that breaks down all our former barriers? Where is the personal, moral, economic, and political transformation that this king and new kingdom usher in? And why were the religious and political rulers so afraid of it? Those are the questions that never get answered in this movie. We witness a gruesome account of the last twelve hours of Jesus' life; we watch him die a hideously painful death; and then we get a whiff of his resurrection. But there is not enough of the kingdom of God here for me. ... We see the suffering, and we may be moved by it. But the film makes it easy to miss the message. The spiritual connection between the two, suffering and kingdom is at the heart of the meaning of Christ's passion.[22]

Both Tom Wright and Jim Wallis react to what they regard as the popular evangelical distortion of the good-news of the kingdom of God. Wright agrees that it is unequivocally the case that there is a personal, spiritual dimension to the Messiah's reign. Every individual's greatest need is for reconciliation with God. But the good news includes more than the personal. Preaching the cross as *The Great Escape* can become a copout from all that the 'kingdom bringer' called us to be and to do.

Wright recommends that we try to visualize what our work-places, homes and churches would look like if God were in charge. We are called to be people through whom 'new creation' happens. The followers of Jesus are invited to be participants in God's great plan to bring about the kingdom 'on earth as it is in heaven'. Creation care is part of kingdom practice. Life in God's kingdom under the Messianic management of Jesus issues in transformed individuals who are passionate not only in reaching out to their friends with God's love. They are also concerned

---

22 Jim Wallis, *Perspectives On The Passion Of The Christ*, (Miramax Books), p.116, 117

to see evidence of the kingdom in their neighbourhoods and their environment. They have grasped the revolutionary nature of Mary's song in which she sings about a God who has a social conscience.

The ushering in of the kingdom is ultimately God's work. That is why we pray for the coming of the kingdom. It is a matter of grace (*gratias* – meaning 'free gift'). That is also why the preaching of the kingdom is good news rather than moralistic advice on how to behave. It is not first and foremost a matter of grinding duty and human achievement. But that does not justify our passivity. God is sovereignly in control but we still have a modest responsibility to share in his reclamation project. The Biblical writers nowhere unravel the conundrum of this double agency. They are not interested in philosophical and metaphysical speculations. They are content to leave the mystery unresolved because it has been unrevealed. God chooses to work in partnership with humans to bring about the kingdom 'on earth as it is in heaven'. God invites us to roll up our sleeves and get to work. As the great early church theologian, St Augustine of Hippo puts it, 'God without us will not; and we without God cannot'. From the day of Pentecost on, the infant church depended entirely on the strength and guidance of the Spirit.

At the other extreme of the 'kingdom-cross' polarity, there are, what Tom Wright calls 'kingdom churches' which seek to make the world a better place but tend to overlook the fact that Jesus is the 'crucified kingdom-bringer'.

In the cause of the kingdom there is always a cost involved. Dietrich Bonhoeffer, the German theologian who died at the hands of the Nazis, wrote of the danger of 'cheap grace'. Grace which costs nothing, Bonhoeffer maintained, ends up counting for nothing and achieving nothing. The Master's call is seriously demanding. Jesus himself did not shrink from strong action which carried the risk of confrontation with the established authorities. His very first provocative action on entering Jerusalem in the first 'holy week' was to enter the Temple as a sign marking the coming of the new Messianic kingdom. The violence he used on that occasion only damaged tables and chairs. As it turned out, it was the kingdom-bringer himself who was violated in Jerusalem. Recruits in his service cannot expect less. They will be subjected to suffering and setbacks. For the young Church deacon Stephen, following the kingdom-bringer meant death by stoning (Acts 7.54-60). In AD 155, Polycarp, the aged bishop of Smyrna courageously went to his death in the stadium uttering the stirring words, 'Eighty and six years have I served him (Christ), and he hath done me no wrong; how then can I blaspheme my king who saved me?'[23] More recently, on the 27th January, 1945, Archbishop Oscar Romero was gunned down at the altar of his cathedral in El Salvador by the ruling elite because he challenged the huge social inequalities in his country. In fearless anticipation of his martyrdom he said, 'A bishop will die, but God's church which is the people, will never perish'. Suffering will always be a mark of Jesus' disciples because as the 'kingdom-bringer' Jesus was both sovereign and vulnerable.

If the kingdom is to take first place in our lives, there will inevitably be a cost. In writing about believers being adopted as God's children, Paul spells out what the implications for the future will be. In Romans chapter 8, he says that the same indwelling Holy Spirit who assures us that we are God's children assures us that we are heirs and the inheritance will include suffering:

> it is that very Spirit bearing witness with our spirit that we are children of God, and if children, then heirs, heirs of God and joint heirs with Christ - if, in fact, we suffer with him so that we may also be glorified with him (Romans 8.16,17).

Scripture lays strong emphasis on the principle that suffering is the path to glory. It was so for the Messiah. It is so for the messianic community also. It is by the way of the cross, along the *via dolorosa*, that the Spirit moves us. The call to be part of the kingdom is not an invitation to modify slightly a few of our worst habits and become glorified social workers. We cannot accept Jesus into our lives as our Saviour from sin

---

23 Bettenson & Maunder, *Documents of the Christian Church*, (Oxford University Press, 1999), 11

and then go back to our former way of life. The New Testament makes the radical nature of the Christian life abundantly clear by its use of many striking metaphors – being 'born anew' (John 3.7), dying, being buried and rising with Christ (Romans 6.3,4). To embrace the gospel is an invitation to die to a whole way of life and to rise to a radically new one. As the hymn writer, Isaac Watts put it in his much loved hymn, 'When I survey the wondrous cross' - 'love so amazing, so divine, demands my soul, my life, my all'.

Maintaining the balance between the cross and the kingdom was a lesson that Simon Peter was slow to learn and in this respect, he is not alone. Still today our churches tend to tip off balance towards one end or the other of the 'kingdom-cross polarity'. They are either passionate about saving souls through evangelism or transforming humanity into the kingdom of God through social action. In either case, they witness to a half gospel. God is the God both of justice and justification.

The cross

When Christians have reflected on the cross, they have done so in two main ways: seeing it as the *answer to the sin problem* and as the *answer to the suffering problem*.

1. The answer to the sin problem - atonement

Although I think that we have much to be thankful for in Tom Wright's emphasis on the relation between the cross and the kingdom, it is when he comes to expound the relation between the cross and sin, that I find him much more problematic. Much of his recent writing is in strong reaction to what has been called the 'punitive gospel'. Wright regards this as a truncated view of atonement framed around the issue of punishment for sin in which a kind, 'good cop' Jesus, stepped in between sinful human beings and a stern 'bad cop' monster God, to bear the penalty that sinners deserve.[24] This view of the cross is expressed in the popular novel, *The Shack*. The three persons of the Trinity are depicted as three individual people living together in a shack in the

---

24 W. Paul Young, *The Shack*, (Windblown Media, 2007), 186

woods. The main character, Mac, speaks for many when he says to Papa (representing God the Father):

> But I always liked Jesus better than you. He seemed so gracious and you seemed so…

To which Papa the 'bad cop' God responds,

> Mean? Sad isn't it? He came to show people who I am and most folks only believe it about him. They still play us off like good cop/ bad cop most of the time, especially the religious folk. When they want people to do what they think is right, they need a stern God. When they need forgiveness, they run to Jesus.

To be fair to Wright, he does concede that the 'punitive gospel' presented by some popular preachers is not one hundred percent wrong and he acknowledges that the best of the Reformers did not present such highly misleading views of the atonement.[25] Yet it is unfortunate, in my opinion, that he has chosen to react to 'caricatures' without providing a fair statement of the position that is being caricatured. As C. S. Lewis somewhere said, 'in judging other faiths or traditions we should always make comparisons between the best exponents of each side rather than the worst'. It is very easy to be beguiled by Tom Wright's flair with language and his obvious passion for the gospel. It has been well said of him that he 'finds it difficult to draft a boring sentence'.[26] He is addictably readable. That only makes it all the more important to carefully critique his presentation.

I, like many others all over the world, am indebted to a former Principal of Ridley College, Melbourne, Leon Morris, for his careful research and writing on the atonement. He consistently reminded his students that the word 'crucial' comes from the word 'crux' or 'cross' and hence, what God achieved on the cross was at the very heart of the good news. Morris delighted in pointing out how the early Christian preachers 'ransacked their vocabulary in order to bring out some small fraction of

---

25 Op.cit., 25
26 D. A. Carson, *Collected Writings on Scripture*, (Crossway, 2010), 283

the mighty thing that God has done for us through the cross.' The early Christian apostles employed a diversity of images for atonement in their preaching without imposing one particular theory as an agreed dogma. They used an image taken from the market place – 'redemption', or from the law courts – 'justification' or even from the pagan temples – 'propitiation'. It is this latter image that has stirred up the recent hostile debate with some accusing those who employ it of 'cosmic child abuse.' But the early Christians were always careful to 'disinfect' the word of its pagan associations. They cleaned up the concept by making important qualifications about the way in which the New Testament preachers used the image.

We have noted above how Tom Wright utilizes a straw-man argument complaining about preachers today who present a picture of a loving Son winning salvation from a stern and unyielding Father. But that is not how the New Testament writers pictured the cross nor is it how the best evangelical preachers present the cross today. Wright is passionate in wanting the Christian 'gospel' to be presented as 'good news'. When Paul preaches the evangel to the Thessalonians he boldly declares:

> you turned to God from idols, to serve a living and true God, and to wait for his Son from heaven, whom he raised from the dead – Jesus, who rescues us from the wrath that is coming (1 Thessalonians 1.9b,10).

Graham Cole is surely right to point out that the 'gospel' is only 'good news' for those who embrace it. Not all do. For them it is bad news indeed. According to Paul, for some it has 'the fragrance of life', but for others 'the smell of death' (2 Corinthians 2:14-16).

Theologians and preachers like Leon Morris took great care *not* to make Christ the object of God's punishment *or* God the object of Christ's persuasion, for both God and Christ were subjects not objects, taking the initiative together to save sinners. There was no unwillingness in either. On the contrary, their wills coincided in the perfect self-sacrifice of love:

All this is from God, who reconciled us to himself through Christ, and has given us the ministry of reconciliation; that is, in Christ God was reconciling the world to himself (2 Corinthians 5:18,19).

The atonement must be understood within a Trinitarian framework. The salvation achieved on the cross is not primarily a 'process,' and even less a 'formula,' but a person, or rather three persons acting with boundless love. It remains a mystery how all of the sin of all humanity could be funnelled into the single event of Jesus' suffering and death. It can never be presented as a mere theory so that we are able to say, 'Oh, so that's it. Now I get it. Now I understand'. To such a response, I would quickly add, in the words of Ben Myers, 'the thing is, if you do, you don't'[27].

Although the cross was a seismic culture shock for the religious and philosophical sensibilities of the first century, its meaning is not to be found in the intensity of Jesus's suffering. As Rowan Williams has said, 'Paul knew that the shock of the cross was not how badly Jesus suffered (what about those who lingered on the cross for days?) … We need, in thinking about the cross, to move beyond the attempt to bring emotions to the boil by pretending that this was, by definition, a uniquely awful form of physical pain'.[28] The Gospel passion narratives dismiss the whole dramatic affair in a few words – 'and they scourged him'; and 'they crucified him.' There was no attempt to embellish the drama as a modern film maker might be tempted to do. The Gospel authors do not want to deflect their readers from the reason for his dying.

I write with some feeling about this teaching on the atonement because it was not through Leon Morris's theoretical exposition of the cross in terms of neat and tidy categories that I most benefited. It was through his pastoral application of the meaning and purpose of Christ's death that I was enabled to continue in ordained ministry for nearly fifty years. A stand-out memory to me is a day in 1964 when I nervously knocked

---

27 This is Ben Myers clever way of referring to the overconfident language employed by some Christians.

28 Edmund Newell (Ed.) *Seven Words for Three Hours*, (DLT, 2005), 28

on Dr Morris's study door at Ridley Theological College, Melbourne. I was a student in training for the ministry. I had come in order to confess something of which I was deeply ashamed. In fact, I felt so ashamed that I thought it required me to abandon my training for ordained ministry. As I entered the room mulling over what I would say and how I would say it, I said to myself, 'I'll bet he's never heard anything like this before!' Two things in particular stand out in my memory.

The first is that he invited me to kneel with him to pray. That might seem unremarkable. Etty Hillesum a Dutch woman who died in Auschwitz in 1943, often referred in her diaries to the importance of this physical gesture. In her diary entry for the 19th July, 1942 she writes about 'kneeling almost naked, in the middle of the floor, completely undone'.[29] Those words describe both her outer posture and her inner state. They sum up exactly how I felt as I knelt with the Principal in the middle of his study floor. My experience on that memorable day gave me an appreciation of the quieter ways of faith which integrate bodily gestures and our anti-God attitudes and actions. The very posture of kneeling helped to foster a sense of transparency and truthfulness. As the novelist Helen Garner has one of her characters Lucy exclaim when confronted with a desperate situation (and no other word fits in describing how I felt that day):

> 'Sometimes there's only one prayer to say. Lamb of God. You take away the sin of the world … Have mercy on us'.[30]

Damage had been done. Somehow, despite my fragmentation, God had taken my failure into Christ. Jesus had paid the price for it. Jesus had absorbed it. This was not mere abstract atonement theology to be mulled over in my head. Kneeling was a vivid way of helping me to appreciate the reality of the wounded love of God as the labour pains bringing forth forgiveness and blotting out my sin from memory. As human beings we do not have total control over our memories. It was especially liberating to be able to rest in the knowledge that God has

---

29 Etty Hillesum, *An Interrupted Life and Letters From Westerbork*, (An Owl Book, 1996), 185
30 Helen Garner, *The Spare Room*, 2008, Text Publishing Melbourne, 100

a wonderful 'forgettery'. In the words of the Old Testament prophet Jeremiah, to which Leon's prayer alluded, God 'remembers our sins no more' (Jeremiah 31.34). When God forgives, God's memory bank is empty. Even though we drive nails through the hands of God, he never stops loving us. Referring to the people of Israel in the Old Testament, Leon Morris wrote:

> There is no way that God will cease to love, not even in the face of the people's unceasing sin. The people sinned and sinned and sinned, but God loved and loved and loved.[31]

In exposing my flawed human nature, the message of the cross became 'good news' indeed for me, a momentous catharsis, consigning my sins to oblivion.

But second, in addition to his prayerful ministry of absolution, helping me to allow Christ to deal with my past, Leon Morris's ministry to me on that memorable day offered the possibility of a different future. I have never forgotten the Bible words that he gave to me as part of the counsel he recommended. They were a paraphrase of the words of Jesus to a would-be follower: 'You have put your hand to the plough and there must be no looking back' (Luke 9.62). God shows us grace not for our own sake, but for other people's. Justification by faith does not work by means of magic. The forgiveness I had received needed to show its fruit in the vocation to which God had called me. I had entered theological college in order to train as an Anglican priest. I must go into the future, faithful to that calling, grateful that my mistakes were not stronger than God's love for me. Yes, God loves me and accepts me as I am but I was challenged to see that that God doesn't leave me as I am. The cross of Jesus stands for the wounded love of God that holds and contains my sins and failures and leads me forward. God loves me into changing and growing. God loves all of us right to our centre of gravity and works from the thing that is unique about each of us. In my case, that, at least in part, was a vocation from which I have derived much pleasure over almost fifty years.

---

31 Leon Morris, *What's a nice church like ours doing in a world like this*, 1983, AIO,66

In the light of this personal experience, I have often reflected that perhaps there would not be so many divisive arguments about the atonement if we appreciated more fully that the climax of the letter to the Romans is not about justification before a Judge. It is about adoption into the Father's family. Jim Packer made the point long ago in his classic book, *Knowing God* when he wrote:

> Justification is a *forensic* idea, conceived in terms of *law*, and viewing God as *judge* ... adoption is a *family* idea, conceived in terms of *love*, and viewing God as *father*.[32]

The high point of Romans is not justification (important and all as it is) but adoption. Closeness, affection, generosity are at the heart of the gospel as Paul expounds it in this great letter. Adoption issuing in fearless freedom and filial prayerfulness is the evidence of the new, rich, full life, described in the climax of the letter:

> For all who are led by the Spirit of God are children of God. For you did not receive a spirit of slavery to fall back again into fear, but you have received a spirit of adoption. When we cry, "Abba! Father!" it is the very spirit bearing witness with our spirit that we are children of God, and if children, then heirs, heirs of God and joint heirs with Christ – if, in fact, we suffer with him so that we may also be glorified with him (Romans 8.14-17).

Freedom not fear rules the adopted child's life. Sometimes we allow ourselves to lapse back into self-salvation, driven by a need to prove ourselves to God. But if we know, deep down in our inner being, that God accepts us - who are we to reject ourselves? Brother Roger, the former Prior of the ecumenical community of Taize in France, never tired of quoting a verse from the first letter of John:

> If our hearts condemn us, God is greater than our hearts (1 John 3.20).

It is God's verdict not ours, that ultimately matters – and yet, we are sometimes tempted to try to prove our worth to God and fall back into a kind of slavery of self-justification.

---

32 J. I. Packer, *Knowing God*, (Hodder & Stoughton, 1973), 187

The Aramaic word *'abba'* was used by Jesus in his agony in the garden of Gethsemane. It is evidently, a term of intimacy, security, unlimited trust, meaning *'daddy'* or *'dear father.'* In Romans 8, Paul goes on to say that this assurance of God's fatherly love is the work of the Spirit. It can be likened to the experience of being hugged by our heavenly Father. It is not always vividly felt and sometimes it is overshadowed by feelings of doubt and despair. But the Spirit sees to it, that confidence in God continues none the less. The Spirit bears witness to us that we are God's children. The tense of the Greek verb is the present continuous tense. Sometimes it might be more intense than at other times but it is an abiding experience nonetheless. John Stott paraphrases the climax of the chapter in this way:

> This is my fixed, unshakable conviction, that neither the crisis of death, nor the calamities of life, nor superhuman agencies, good or bad ('angels, principalities, powers'), nor time (whether present or future), nor space (whether height or depth), 'nor anything else in all creation' will be able, however hard it may try, 'to separate us from the love of God in Christ Jesus our Lord' – the love historically displayed in the death of Christ; the love of God poured into our hearts by the Spirit of Christ (Romans 8.38,39).[33]

2. The answer to the problem of suffering – theodicy

In addition to dealing with our sins, another way of viewing the cross has risen to prominence because of the litany of terrors produced over the past hundred years: the trenches of the First World War, fifty five million dead in the Second World War, Auschwitz, Hiroshima, the killing fields of Cambodia, Kosovo, Rwanda, September 11, Iraq, Afghanistan and Syria and more recently, the jihadi recruitment of ISIS. In the light of these endless horrors, many theologians have viewed the cross as an answer, in part, to the problem of innocent suffering – referred to in theological jargon as theodicy.

As we have seen, atonement seeks to answer the question as to how humanity can be justified before a holy God in the face of sin. Theodicy,

---

33 John Stott, *Men Made New*, (IVF, 1966), 106

on the other hand, asks how God can be justified to humanity in the face of appalling human suffering. The cross is presented as the answer to the suffering problem.

God incarnate wept human tears and knew pain and grief from inside the human condition. Graham Cole rightly points out that: 'The God of biblical portrayal is no remote frozen absolute without emotion'.[34] It is possible to have thoughts of God that are too human. But we can also err by having thoughts of God that are not human enough. It is far more credible to believe that God does care about human suffering when he himself demonstrated his love by sharing in our suffering through taking the human condition and suffering a cruel death. And those who see themselves as the victims of evil will look at the Cross of Jesus with very different eyes from those who see themselves as the responsible agents of evil. 'God and crucifixion, God and suffering, God and humiliation, God and grief and pain, God and tragedy: these are not exclusive opposites'.[35]

In his Narnia tales, C. S. Lewis was able to depict the Christ-like figure of Aslan with human empathy. In *The Magician's Nephew*, Digory goes hunting through new worlds to try to find something to cure his mother, who was dying of tuberculosis. When he meets Aslan it seems that all his hopes have gone. He becomes aware of his own wrongdoing and that he has to try to atone. He blurts out,

> But please, please – won't you – can't you give me something that will cure mother?

> Up till then he had been looking at the Lion's great front feet and the huge claws on them; now, in despair, he looked up at its face. What he saw surprised him as much as anything in his whole life. For the tawny face was bent down near his own and (wonder of wonders) great shining tears stood in the Lion's eyes. They were such big, bright tears compared with Digory's own that for a moment he felt as if the Lion must really be sorrier about his mother than he was himself.[36]

---

34 Graham Cole, *God the Peacemaker*, 2009, IVP, 257
35 Richard Bauckham & Trevor Hart, *At the Cross*, 1999, IVP, 100
36 C. S. Lewis, *The Magicians Nephew*, (HarperCollins, 1995), 139, 140

In situations of suffering, Jesus cares far, far more than we can, or we can imagine caring. He has bright tears for the child with cancer, for the child killed in war, whoever the aggressor, for the child born with the handicap.

If the chief concern of a theory of atonement is with how we can be made acceptable to God, the chief concern of theodicy is how God can be made acceptable to us. In fact, the two approaches are not really alternatives. They are complimentary and need to be integrated.

Recently however, there has developed a reaction to this new way of understanding the cross. It is known as 'anti-theodicy'. Theodicies it is claimed tend to be Enlightenment projects, attempting to solve the unsolvable. When life appears to be crumbling into oblivion, it is not pat philosophical explanations but candid lament, enabled by the Spirit that can best help the person in the depth of loneliness and suffering. Richard Bauckham, as an admirer of the great German theologian, Jurgen Moltmann, would probably not describe his theology of the cross in terms of 'anti-theodicy'.[37] However, his theology of the cross does resonate with this newer understanding with its appreciation of the place of lament in our lives, especially during times of suffering. Bauckham recognizes that our culture does not enable people to face radical evil and meaningless tragedy. It gives people no way of crying out to God, or for God, or even against God. In the no-longer-felt-absence of God, people are allowed to have only problems that can be solved.

The crucified God solves no problems. To find God's presence in God's absence is not a solution to a problem. It is, claims Bauckham, something infinitely more important. If Jesus' cry of dereliction, of god-forsakenness, is silenced, where, he asks, is the point of connection to our pain? In a Good Friday meditation written for the English *Church Times* paper, Bauckham tellingly cites the Italian theologian, Gerard Rosse: 'Jesus in his abandonment is the God of all those without God'.[38]

---

37 See Richard J. Bauckham, *Moltmann – Messianic Theology in the Making*, (Marshall Morgan and Scott, 1987).
38 Richard Bauckham, *'He hung and suffered there'*, Church Times, 4 April, 1996, 12

This is what the story of Good Friday surely says to a culture that is consumer oriented. In Ben Myer's passionate words, 'We must trust – trust that the God who forsakes us is the God who is with us. Here is a faith with nothing in it for me – but Him. Him. Only Him. Truly Him. Always Him'.[39]

Stephen Torr, a British Pentecostal theologian, has suggested how that momentous step might be taken. He recognizes that the presence of the Spirit is not only evident in 'feel-good' experiences when people dance and sway in worship. There are times in our life when sadness is warranted, and happiness would be totally out of place. Sometimes discouraged and depressed people are deeply filled with the Spirit. Torr writes:

> What the Bible seems to suggest as a significant answer to the problem of innocent and meaningless suffering is to lament – to speak honestly to God with all the rawness of emotion that such honesty demands. God doesn't call for yes women![40]

We only have to note how Israel employed psalms of lament during their exile in Babylon crying out: 'where are You, God?' or 'How long, O Lord?' Often their prayers were not very polite to God and they felt it was OK be angry with him. Jesus himself died with the psalms of lament on his lips. In the garden of Gethsemane his prayer moved from disorientation to re-orientation – 'Abba, Father, for you all things are possible; remove this cup from me; yet, not what I want, but what you want' (Mark 14.36). On the cross he quoted the first verse of psalm 22, 'My God, my God, why have you abandoned me'.

And as was the case with our Lord, so too, Paul tells us in Romans 8, that we as adopted children, can invoke the Spirit's help in our suffering. 'The Spirit intercedes with sighs too deep for words' (Romans 8.26,27). Some Pentecostal scholars see this Spirit inspired prayer taking the form of glossolalia or 'speaking in tongues'. But whether or not the reference is to ecstatic speech, it is clear from this passage that the Spirit

---

39 The closing words of a sermon for Good Friday by Ben Myers.
40 Stephen C. Torr, *A Dramatic Pentecostal/Charismatic Anti-Theodicy*, (Pickwick, 2013)

offers help during 'dark nights of the soul' when believers find it hard to pray. Some Pentecostal Christians tend to suppress lamentation and emphasize the place of the psalms of joy and praise with a Colgate smile! But happy thoughts are not always the best medicine. Nor are intellectual explanations what most people need during periods of suffering. This is why Torr prefers the term 'anti-theodicy' to describe the way the cross addresses the problem of suffering. His position can be illustrated by the experience of Professor Frances Young who has a severely handicapped son, Arthur. For years she has struggled with the theodicy questions raised by Arthur's birth. Release for her came not *via* theological explanations. The questions remain. It was an 'anti-theodicy' experience of the Spirit that changed her perception. She wrote:

> The moment remains vivid; I remember precisely what chair I was sitting in, that I was sitting on the edge of it, ready to get up and go and do something in the kitchen, when a 'loud thought' came into my head: 'It doesn't make any difference to me whether you believe in me or not.' I had a sense of being stunned, of being put in my place. Nothing dramatic happened, but since that moment I have not seriously doubted God's reality. God confronted me as utter otherness.[41]

We tend to trap God in our own questions. When theodicies fail to satisfy, what is needed according to Stephen Torr, is a cross-shaped pneumatology, a constant *epiclesis*, calling on the Spirit of God – 'Come Holy Spirit'. 'Come and intercede for us with sighs too deep for words'. Such a prayer is a celebration, not a denial, of life as it really is.

The resurrection

Death inspires terror in many people. Woody Allen expressed his angst in relation to death when he quipped: 'It's not that I'm afraid to die. I just don't want to be there when it happens!' The process of dying is often messy and undignified. But because Jesus Christ has personally

---

41 Frances Young, *God's Presence: A Contemporary Recapitulation of Early Christianity*, (Cambridge University Press, 2013), 385

conquered death, Christians celebrate the resurrection as God's '*eu-catastrophe*'. They defiantly sing the words of St Paul:

Where, O death, is your victory?
Where, O death, is your sting? (1 Cor.15.55).

A funeral is therefore, a time for reminding ourselves of the unshakeable hope of the resurrection. But it also a time for grieving and we should not be afraid of that. If Jesus wept at the grave of his friend Lazarus, why should we not grieve? (John 11.35) Death separates us from our loved ones and it is frequently painful. No amount of floral arrangements can disguise the pain. Death is no friend. Paul calls it an enemy (1 Corinthians 15.26). There are some Christians who see the absence of any show of grief as evidence of a 'strong faith'. They think that the norm for Christians should be a 'joyous funeral'. Tears of grief are regarded as being signs of emotional immaturity or spiritual weakness. Christians do not 'grieve as others who have no hope' but we still grieve. St Augustine made this point well when he wrote, 'We are tossed on a tide that puts us to the proof and if we could not sob our troubles in your ear, what hope should we have left to us?'

When we come to consider the historical evidence for God's victory over death in the resurrection of Jesus we are confronted with a paradox. Because orthodox Christianity claims that the resurrection is something that really happened, it must open itself to the scrutiny of historians. That is a risk that authentic Christianity must take. After all, if it did not take place in history, then as Paul wrote, the Christian faith is an empty shell (1Corithians 15.14). For Paul and the other New Testament writers, the resurrection of Jesus is regarded as the defining and indispensable foundation of the Christian faith.

On the other hand, because the resurrection is a unique action of God, it is not susceptible of historical proof. Historians may conceivably lead to the conclusion that the tomb was empty. But that is about as far as an historian can go in the capacity of a technical historian. The resurrection itself defies historical investigation. The same sort of paradox confronts historians when they examine other major Christian concepts such as the incarnation and the crucifixion. Jesus' birth was normal and historians can enquire into the place and date of his birth but as historians they have no way of either affirming or denying a virgin conception. Again, when it comes to the crucifixion, historians may agree that on a certain day in the early years of our era Jesus did in fact die on a cross. But the early Christian preachers were not interested in the cross merely as a brute fact of history. They proclaimed its saving significance. In each of these three major events in Jesus' life - conception, saving death and resurrection - we are confronted with events that took place on just one occasion. As such, they fall outside the domain of historical investigation. All that the historian, working as an historian can conclude is: something strange happened, we just don't know what! Historians don't know about resurrections. It is quite unlike anything else that has ever occurred in history and therefore beyond the historian's capability of finally nailing down. The resurrection was proclaimed as a 'uniquely unique'[42] event, a divine incursion into human history. 'God has made him both Lord and Messiah, this Jesus whom you crucified' (Acts 2.36).

Such is the paradox that confronts us in the resurrection. It both *demands* historical investigation and at the same time, *defies* historical investigation. Some scholars resolve the paradox by adopting a sceptical view of the Gospels. Others retain a robust view of revelation by taking both sides of this paradox seriously. A good example of this latter approach is the ground-breaking book by Richard Bauckham *Jesus and the Eyewitnesses* which won the prestigious Michael Ramsey prize in 2009. Bauckham cannot easily be pigeon-holed. Is he a radical or a conservative? The judges described the book as 'orthodox but novel' a description which probably means that neither conservative nor liberal scholars are entirely satisfied!

For example, the conservative Evangelical scholar, Andreas J. Kostenberger, is disturbed by Bauckham's innovative suggestion that the author of John's Gospel was not the apostle John, the son of Zebedee, as has traditionally been maintained. Instead, Bauckham argues that the author is the mysterious 'one whom Jesus loved' mentioned several

---

42 A descriptor employed by Bauckham derived from the writing on hermeneutics by Paul Ricoeur.

times in the Gospel. He suggests that this, in part, accounts for the fourth Gospel's very different style from the Synoptic Gospels. Matthew, Mark and Luke are largely drawn from sources in and around Galilee. John, he claims, draws on a circle of followers from Jerusalem, such as the 'beloved Disciple'. Furthermore, Bauckham tentatively suggests that he was the owner of the house in Jerusalem where the Last Supper took place. He certainly was in a prominent position at the table, leaning close to Jesus at the last Supper (John 13.23). The fourth century theologian, Hilary of Poitiers, interpreted the image of the 'beloved disciple' resting his head on Jesus' chest as 'listening to the heartbeat of God'. According to the Fourth Evangelist, the 'beloved disciple' appears to have been our Lord's most intimate friend. Far from regarding John's Gospel as being unreliable, historically and theologically, as popular liberal writers, such as Marcus Borg have argued, Bauckham claims that the 'beloved disciple', as one of the major sources of John's Gospel, gives the Gospel historical and theological credibility. He was closest to Jesus and therefore able to see furthest into the meaning of the events described. He tells the story of Jesus so that we can see both *the events as he saw them* and *the meaning he came to see in them* - 'we are beneficiaries of both this witnesses' *sight* and his *insight'*. In summary form, we could say that Bauckham's conclusions about the authorship of the Fourth Gospel are both traditional and novel. He does not please either those in the conservative camp (like Kostenberger) or the liberal camp (like Borg).

In challenging the conclusions of Form criticism the book drops a bombshell into New Testament studies. Since the 1960's, the findings of the Form critics have held sway in much New Testament study. Arguing that the Gospels are the product of anonymous early church tradition which circulated in definite oral forms, these critics frequently ended up with a reductionist Jesus, challenging the credibility of the Gospels.

Contrary to this entire argument about the material in the Gospels resting on anonymous tradition, Bauckham claims that much of the Gospel material goes back to named eyewitness sources. In addition to the unnamed 'beloved disciple' he builds his case on such things as the importance of the lists naming the twelve disciples, who were regarded as the official eyewitnesses and guarantors of the content of the message. He also sites a host of other named individuals in the Gospels, who, it is argued, provided testimony to the events narrated (why otherwise name them?) – people like Cleopas; the named women at the cross and the tomb of Jesus; Simon of Cyrene and his sons; and the named recipients of Jesus' healing ministry such as Jairus and Bartimaeus. It is not for nothing that verbs of seeing come thick and fast in the Gospels so that at the cross, Mark tells us, 'there were also women *looking on* from a distance; among them were Mary Magdalene, and Mary the mother of James the younger and of Joses, and Salome'. For good reason, the primacy of sight is emphasized.[43] This is not material that circulated anonymously. It is eyewitness testimony and by its very nature testimony asks to be trusted. Of course, this trust should never be uncritical. At the same time, contemporary readers must acknowledge that they cannot verify for themselves everything that the witnesses claim. As Bauckham points out,

> Testimony is irreducible; we cannot, at least in some of its most distinctive and valuable claims go behind it and make our own autonomous verification of them.[44]

In the light of this argument, what is needed as we read the Gospels is not a *'hermeneutic of suspicion'* but a *'hermeneutic of trust'*. Andrew Louth presses the point further when he says,

> We become Christians by becoming members of the Church, by trusting our forefathers (*sic*) in the faith. If we cannot trust the Church to have understood Jesus then we have lost Jesus: and the resources of modern scholarship will not help us to find him.[45]

We can be confident that in the accounts of the resurrection we have struck a genuine historical seam in the gospel bedrock. But the resurrection does not lock Christ in history. It sets him free to be the

---

43 See Bauckham, *The Gospels as Eyewitness Testimony*, (Grove Biblical Series B 48), 11
44 Richard Bauckham, *The Gospels as Eyewitness Testimony*, (Grove Biblical Series, B 48) 22
45 Andrew Louth, *Discerning the Mystery*, (Oxford: Clarendon Press, 1983) 93

contemporary for all future generations. As a young person I loved to join in singing the rousing chorus:

'He lives; He lives; Christ Jesus lives today
He walks with me and talks with me along life's narrow way'.

Is this chorus overstating the case? I can recall returning home from Easter youth camps with its words reverberating in my head, and leading me to think that in the living Jesus I had a friend who could be known just like any of my other friends. Usually however, when I got home, life all too quickly fell back to a fairly low-octane level of spiritual energy. Was it just the normal flatness to be expected after a mountain-top experience? Or was there something in my expectation-laden singing that set me up for a fall? Is our experience of the risen Lord just like our experience of our friends with whom we 'walk and talk along life's narrow ways'? Much of the popular rhetoric in hymns and choruses gives the impression that Our Lord is still with us in the way that he was with Mary Magdalene in the garden or Cleopas and his companion as they journeyed on the Emmaus Road.

However it is important to notice that Mary Magdalene is told not to cling to Jesus because he is on the way to the Father. 'Do not hold on to me, because I have not yet ascended to the Father' (John 20.17). This was a moment of transition. We have to take Jesus' departure seriously. We cannot draw a straight line from the Gospels to our situation today. Many readers of the Bible fail to take into account the obvious difference between our circumstances and the circumstances of those involved in the Biblical narrative. But that difference must always be borne in mind in interpreting the gospels. The risen Lord is now at the right hand of the Father, not with us on earth. That is why Paul urges us to 'seek the things that are above, where Christ is, seated at the right hand of God' (Col. 3.1). We live on the other side of the ascension. Of course, there is a sense in which we can say he is with us by means of the Spirit. But without that qualification, we can too easily give the impression that Jesus is accessible to us in exactly the same way as any other human person we know. He is not. Human beings relate to one another through their bodies. Psychologists have even developed a term for this form of communication, calling it 'body language'. This is one of the main reasons why many of us find persevering in prayer so difficult. God is the only unembodied person with whom we claim to talk.[46]

We cannot use the 'sightings' of the risen Lord as prescriptions for our own experience. The words of the risen Lord to Thomas have application to us: 'Have you believed because you have seen me? Blessed are those who have not seen and yet have come to believe' (John 20.29). The benediction is promised to those who have come to believe by interacting with Jesus' covenanted words. We are to enjoy the *reality* of his presence but we are to beware of the *rhetoric*. The *rhetoric* can too easily set us up for disappointment and disillusionment. Throughout the history of the church, people have testified to hearing the audible voice of Jesus or seeing him in a vision. Such mystical experiences may well be authentic. If they are, they are uncovenanted, un-promised gifts and should be received with gratitude. They may equally be fantasy and that is why all religious experiences require theological scrutiny. How then, can we who 'walk now by faith and not by sight' (2 Corinthians 5.7), come to know the risen, reigning, returning Lord for ourselves? John Stott answers this question by telling a story passed on to him by Donald Coggan, a former Archbishop of Canterbury:

There was a sculptor once, so they say, who sculpted a statue of our Lord. And people came from great distances to see it – Christ in all his strength and tenderness. They would walk all around the statue, trying to grasp its splendour, looking at it now from this angle, now from that. Yet still its grandeur eluded them, until they consulted the sculptor himself. He would invariably reply 'There's only one angle from which this statue can be truly seen. *You must kneel.*'[47]

---

46 I am indebted for much of what I have shared in this paragraph to an article written many years ago by Dr Graham Cole, entitled: *Experiencing the Lord: Rhetoric and Reality.*
47 Quoted in John Stott, *The Incomparable Christ,* (IVP, 2001), 235

Questions for reflection

1. How important is saying the Creed in the liturgy for you? Do you think it is helpful to regard the creeds as a kind of conceptual map?

2. How might we acknowledge our tendencies towards the *holiness of the Pharisees* who withdrew from those considered 'unclean' or 'other' rather than the *holiness of Jesus* who spread wholeness? With whom do we find ourselves spending time?

3. 'The Biblical writers make no distinction between the 'natural' and the 'supernatural world.' For them, nothing is 'natural' in the sense that it happens by itself. God is involved and active in everything – in the routine events as well as the remarkable events.' What is the importance of this observation?

4. Do you think that there is a need in the church for a 'revolution of rising expectations' as we prepare for worship? Should we expect healings to occur?

5. Where do you think that your church sits on the 'kingdom-cross' polarity?

6. The atonement is often framed around the issue of punishment for sin in which a kind, 'good cop' Jesus, stepped in between sinful human beings and a stern 'bad cop' monster God, to bear the penalty that sinners deserve. Why is this view a caricature of the atonement as presented in the New Testament?

7. We tend to trap God in our own questions. When theodicies fail to satisfy, what is needed is a cross-shaped pneumatology, a constant *epiclesis*, calling on the Spirit of God – 'Come Holy Spirit'. 'Come and intercede for us with sighs too deep for words'. Do you think that this approach is more pastoral than offering explanations as to why a good God allows suffering?

8. Reading the Gospel accounts of the resurrection requires a 'hermeneutic of trust' rather than a 'hermeneutic of suspicion'. Do you agree?

Prayer

Creator God, we are all different, mirroring the wonders of your creation. We approach you with different attitudes – some eager, some reluctant, some understanding, some misunderstanding. In your love, you have given us Jesus so that we might encounter you in one like us. Deal with us according to our differences; our strengths and our weaknesses so that we may come increasingly to know you in Him, through the same Jesus Christ our Lord. Amen[48]

---

48 I owe this prayer to Bishop David Farrer who used it in a Retreat for the clergy of Newcastle diocese.

5. The Unfolding Story of the Church

Michael Ramsey was one of the great 20th Century Anglo-Catholic theologians. In his classic book *The Gospel and the Catholic Church* he expounded an ecclesiology (study of the Church, '*ecclesia*') that identifies the church as the 'extension of the incarnation'. It represented a very high view of the church. But it was also a view fraught with dangers, dangers that have become more apparent in recent times with the widespread scandal of clergy child abuse. Clearly, the church is a human institution and it is important to distinguish Christ from the church. The church is fallen in a way that Christ is not. More thinking was needed about the true nature of ecclesiology.

In due course, fresh thinking on the nature of the church came to fruition with one of Michael Ramsey's successors, Rowan Williams, himself an admirer of Ramsey. In his brilliant book about the theology of Rowan Williams entitled, *Christ the Stranger*, Benjamin Myers tells a story about a certain German theologian who once remarked that he does not go to church on Sunday mornings. Instead, he lies in his hammock and ponders ecclesiology. Myers then goes on to make the following comment:

> Is this not the gravest temptation for so many theologians – to imagine the church as a spiritual ideal, a sort of Platonic form of ecclesiality, instead of the disappointingly earthy experience of embodied human community? To stay in your hammock thinking about ecclesiology: that is a recipe not for ecclesiology but for angelology. Rowan Williams thinks that Christ came to create a community not of angels but of real human beings. That is where his view of the church differs from so many others: there are no wings in Williams' theology.[1]

Michael Ramsey's view of the church was too elevated. The church is not the incarnate Son. Rowan William's view of the church, no doubt

---

1 Benjamin Myers, *Christ the Stranger: The Theology of Rowan Williams*, (T&T Clark, 2012), 20

coloured by the turmoil over gay sexuality in the Anglican Communion, left him with a view that was a long way from the angels! The truth probably lies somewhere between these two great Anglo-Catholic bishop-theologians. The idea of the 'pure' church is a chimera. Moments of glorious generosity, wisdom and bold witness coexist alongside a great deal of unfaithfulness, gossip and corruption. Commitment to being part of such a community requires 'grit and gumption'. None of us gets the church on our own terms. We can apply the words of Woody Allen to our membership of the church and say, 'Ninety percent of church life consists of turning up'! But in turning up, we must make the further commitment to do all that we can to reduce the gap between the *ideal* and the *actual*. Often that will mean a change of heart for us. As St Augustine is reputed to have said, 'If I seek the church's enemies, I must not look *without* but *within*'.

Of the four Gospel writers, it is Luke alone who goes on to write a second volume, the Acts of the Apostles. In his first volume he gives an account of 'all that Jesus began to do and teach'. In his second volume he gives an account of 'all that the risen, ascended Jesus continued to do and to teach through the working of the Holy Spirit'. It ought not to surprise us that some prefer to speak of 'The Acts of the Apostles' as 'The Acts of the Holy Spirit'. In the early chapters of that second volume, Luke provides several little vignettes or ideal sketches of the fledgling church in Jerusalem. These cameos of the church do not imply that Luke is an *idealist*. He is a *realist* and knows that the church always contains people who are not Christians or who would like to be Christians or have stopped being Christians. In Acts chapter 5 he recounts the story of Ananias and Sapphira who withheld money from the apostles. It has been said that for Luke, they are portrayed as 'the patron saints of church thieves'. Yet even so, Luke remains firm in his conviction that the Christian life is not a life lived *solo*. The Christian faith is intended to be *personal* but not *individualistic*. How can we learn to love if no one else is around? How can we learn kindness or gentleness or goodness in isolation? How can we learn patience unless someone puts ours to the test? As attractive as solitary sanctification may seem, it is life amid people with all their imperfections that develops many of the qualities God requires.

Kevin J. Vanhoozer poses a vital question for those already inside the church to consider. He asks, 'What has the church to say and do that no other institution can say or do?' In his little cameos or sketches of the church, Luke provides clues to answer Vanhoozer's important question. Taken together, these vignettes provide a blueprint for the churches life. They featured four defining characteristics:

A learning community

They devoted themselves to the apostles' teaching (Acts 2.42).

John Stott writing about the coming of the Spirit on the Day of Pentecost in Acts 2 says:

> One might perhaps say that the Holy Spirit opened a school in Jerusalem that day; its teachers were the apostles whom Jesus had appointed; and there were 3,000 pupils in the kindergarten![2]

If God is to be worshipped in Spirit and in truth, then knowledge is crucial (John 4.24). In this regard it is important to notice that the new converts on the day of Pentecost were not enjoying a mystical experience which led them to despise their mind or disdain theology. Bishop Handley Moule of Durham warned that the Christian: 'must beware equally of 'untheological' devotion and of 'un-devotional' theology.'

In our post-modern culture many people are sceptical of truth claims. In his speaking, Stott sometimes made reference to Christians who were 'keen but clueless'. He was always careful to assert that 'anti-intellectualism and the fullness of the Spirit are mutually incompatible, because the Holy Spirit is the Spirit of truth'.[3] Churches that are doctrine-lite have been likened to the little pig who built his house of straw. When the wolf blows, the house will simply vanish in the wind. To quote Ben Myers again:

---

2 John R.W. Stott, *The Message of Acts*, (IVP, 1990), 82
3 Ibid, 82

A faith that doesn't ask questions, including questions about itself, to keep itself honest, free from hypocrisy, cliché, and guff is an unworthy faith. And a faith that won't engage in dialogue with other Christians, with people of other faiths, with people with no faith at all – this kind of faith is either pathetically insecure or it's hiding something. And a church that doesn't encourage such open, probing conversations will be a dumbed-down and finally ignorant church and not the culture of listening and learning it is called to be.[4]

Many of the newer 'emergent' churches tend to be doctrinal minimalists. But when our knowledge of God's truth is diminished, our understanding of God is diminished and no amount of contrived mystery by gathering in dim, flickering candlelight can compensate for this loss. The overculture in which the churches now operate is so strong that unless there is robust and relevant teaching and preaching in our churches they will not survive the onslaught.

We must also notice that the early disciples didn't imagine that, 'because they had received the Spirit, the Spirit was the only teacher they needed and they could dispense with human teachers. On the contrary, they sat at the apostle's feet, hungry to receive instruction, and they persevered in it'.[5] The teaching role of the church ought to be regarded as a priority for clergy. It could hardly be more forcibly expressed than it has been by J. I. Packer when he says, 'Priority one is to teach, priority two is to teach, and priority three is to teach. We clergy should have a conscience whereby we ask ourselves at the end of each day, "What teaching have I done today? To whom have I taught what?"'[6] Confronted with new and complex moral questions which divide our communities, priests and pastors need to be helping their people to adopt the attitude of the Beroeans in Acts 17, who 'examined the scriptures every day to see whether these things were so' (Acts 17.11).

No doubt all of us in our fallen state are a mixture of orthodoxy and heterodoxy. Commenting on those who think that they are always

---

4 In a sermon on Mark 4.35-41
5 Ibid, 82
6 J. I. Packer, *The Centrality of Holy Scripture in Anglicanism*, (Crux, vol. XI, No. 1, 2004) 17

orthodox and sound and have nothing to learn from those who take a different perspective on the faith, Tom Wright has quipped, 'we like to think that orthodoxy is my "doxy" and heterodoxy is some-one else's "doxy"! While Christians have a core commitment to the Bible, vibrant debate on the implications of the Bible is part of what makes us healthy – 'iron sharpens iron'. There is a certain exclusive, sectarian-like mentality which is always withdrawing in search of a purer church. We cannot expect to settle into the church as if it were a warm bath. Our commitment must be to the actually existent church of today.

As well as *orthodoxy in truth* there needs to be *orthopraxy in behaviour*. In his second letter to Timothy Paul writes:

All Scripture is inspired by God and is useful for teaching, for reproof, for correction, and for training in righteousness, so that everyone who belongs to God may be proficient, *equipped for every good work* (2 Tim 3:16,17).

The first part of that passage stresses the divine origin of the Scriptures. They are literally 'exhaled by God' – 'breathed out by God'. Despite their divine origin however, the personalities of the human authors was not obliterated. God did not treat them as fax-machines into which a message was dropped directly from heaven. Despite their human frailties and failures, God was able to get across what he wanted to communicate to the human race. But of equal importance to the divine origin of the Scriptures, is the whole purpose of Bible study – *'so that everyone who belongs to God may be proficient, equipped for every good work'*.

Christians are 'do-gooders' however much that term brings scorn and ridicule from others. Bible study that does not lead to concrete behavioural changes aborts what God designs the Bible to give birth to. 'Truth' in the New Testament is not simply a matter of the mind. 'Those who *do* what is true come to the light' (John 3:21). The truth is to be lived and seen and embodied. It is orthopraxy as well as orthodoxy. It involves *deeds* as well as *creeds*. As Gandhi famously said, 'I would become a Christian if I could see one'.

A caring community

Today the lines of communication between people are more numerous than ever before; e-mail, text-messaging and cell phones are pervasive in our culture. We are in touch with everyone potentially, but we know and are known by almost no one in particular. Being part of an authentic community was vital to the early Christians. The Greek word for 'community' is *'koinonia'* and it is derived from the word, *'koinos'*, meaning 'common'. The early church *shared things in common* and they *shared out of their abundance with those in need.*

First, *'koinonia'* as what the church *'shares in together'*. This is the very being of God, for 'our fellowship (*'koinonia'*) is with the Father and with his Son, Jesus Christ' (1 John 1.3). Similarly, at the end of his second letter to the Corinthians Paul gives the words, known popularly by Christians as the Grace: 'The grace of the Lord Jesus Christ, the love of God, and the communion *('koinonia')* of the Holy Spirit be with all of you' (2Corinthians 13.13). *'Koinonia'* is a Trinitarian experience, catching believers up in the mutual love between the three persons of the Trinity. As someone has remarked, 'Before there was a sin for God to hate, he always had a Son to love'. Some Christians, impatient with doctrine and dogma, assume that the doctrine of the Trinity is a piece of theological lumber that we can get on very happily without. But in fact, it is a doctrine which has powerful application to our church life. The Trinity as an ec-static communion of persons, gives a vision of a community that can embrace difference and yet hold together in unity. God is a divine community-in-mission who calls the church to be a community-in-mission.

It is no accident that so many of the commands given in the New Testament letters involve *'one another'*: welcome one another; care for one another; bear with one another; forgive one another; submit to one another; admonish one another; exhort one another, and so on. The reason for all these varied injunctions is quite obvious: clearly, *we need one another*!

Yet, sadly, our churches are too often places of bickering and backbiting - *'See how these Christians hate one another!'* There have always been gossipers in the church. In his first letter to Timothy, Paul refers to those who 'are not merely idle, but also gossips and busybodies, saying what they should not say' (1 Timothy 5.13). We need to pay attention to our 'speech ethics'. Robert Banks has said, 'today, gossip in the church has become a full time industry! .... We seem to be part of a "nudge nudge wink wink" church. We are eager to cut people down to size. We lap up scandal. We are often ready to believe the worst. Much of what passes for news today is simply gossip'. Speech ethics in the contemporary church, especially in the debates surrounding 'marriage equality', urgently require the development of corporate protocols that will enable honest and courteous debate with truth as the goal for all concerned. Individual strategies are also required, such as asking ourselves whether we are willing, if necessary, to say face to face, what we are willing to say behind another's back. James warns of the harm that can be caused by unsubstantiated rumours. He writes: 'the tongue is a small member, yet it boasts of great exploits. How great a forest is set ablaze by a small fire! And the tongue is a fire' (James 3.5,6). 'There a low-risk and high-risk times for forest fires.'[7] When the ground is well-watered, the risk is low; when it is dry, the risk is high. Much the same applies in the faith community. Where there is a living spiritual freshness, gossip and unsubstantiated rumour will not go far; but among people who are spiritually dry, the tongue's spark will quickly create a fire – a fire that will spread fast to other dry people, causing damage and destruction.

People outside the church are put off by our divisions and our readiness to make more. It is rightly said that, 'divisions in the church breed atheism in the world'. By contrast, the early church was known for its love and outsiders noticed and would comment: 'see how these Christians *love one another*'. Many years ago, Bruce Larson spoke of the need for authentic community by comparing the church today with what was on offer at an English pub. He wrote:

> The neighbourhood bar is possibly the best counterfeit there is to the fellowship Christ wants to give his Church. It's an imitation, dispensing liquor instead of grace, escape rather than reality, but it is

---

7 In a lecture given at St John's Camberwell by Richard Bauckham.

a permissive, accepting and inclusive fellowship. It is unshockable. It is democratic. You can tell people secrets and they usually don't tell others or even want to. The bar flourishes not because most people are alcoholics, but because God has put into the human heart the desire to know and be known, to love and be loved, and so many seek a counterfeit at the price of a few beers. Christ wants His church to be unshockable, democratic and permissive - a fellowship where people can come in and say 'I'm sunk!' 'I'm beat!' 'I've had it!' Alcoholics Anonymous has this quality. Our churches too often miss it.[8]

Sometimes the church is exclusively orientated around the nuclear family. For a childless couple, the rituals and rhetoric of the church on occasions such as 'mothering Sunday' can be insensitive and painful. Giving an infertile mother a bouquet of flowers can feel like receiving a bunch of 'pity flowers'. One mother struggling with childlessness found going to church hard. She said,

> It feels as though the family unit is something that is celebrated a lot, and it makes you feel as though you're lacking in some way. I found secular environments so much easier to be in. At work, I felt quite normal: a lot of people get married later, and don't have children. Work was often like a retreat: church was stressful.[9]

Similarly, many churches require single people to embrace celibacy and then guarantee them a life of loneliness. Those who are single, for whatever reason, need to be embraced by friendship. Jesus expanded the concept of family, taking it beyond the bloodline, when he said to Peter:

> Truly I tell you, there is no one who has left house or brothers or sisters or mother or father or children or fields, for my sake and the sake of the good news, who will not receive a hundredfold now in this age – houses, brothers and sisters, mothers and children, and fields and persecutions – and in the age to come eternal life (Mark 10.29,30).

A twentieth century liberation theologian, Juan Luis Segundo defined the church as 'an undreamed of possibility for love'.[10] Yet many turn

---

8 Quoted in John Stott, *One People*, (Falcon, 1969), 70
9 Church Times, London, May, 2015, 24
10 Richard Lennan, *Risking the Church*, (Oxford University Press, 2004), 53

away from our churches not because of the message but because of the lack of relational authenticity they find among church members, where the relationships are pseudo-relationships and there is pseudo-community. One bishop encouraged his clergy to concentrate on prayer and parties. Jesus was a party goer and many of his parables were about feasting together. If we do not embody the faith, if we are not an authentic community, we undermine all our efforts at outreach. To paraphrase Paul's great poem on love in 1 Corinthians 13: 'we may undertake all the best re-structuring plans possible and craft superb mission programs but without love, we have gained nothing'. As a church we are called into and caught up in the whole venture of loving the world as God loves it. Referring to one of the sayings of the early desert Fathers, Rowan Williams has said:

> We only love God as much as the person we love least. We do not go to God without each other. We go to heaven in each other's pockets.

It is not difficult to see how this early desert monasticism has impacted on Williams own deep convictions about the nature of the church. In the thick of all the Anglican shenanigans over the issue of homosexuality he gave a lecture on ecclesiology in which he said:

> If Christ is risen and the church is catholic, then there can be no 'sides' and the church's role is to dismantle the whole logic of side-taking.[11]

This does not mean that the insights of individuals should be disregarded. Individuality of thought needs to be prized alongside due regard for community. There is a continuing need for prophetic (reminding) thought. In stressing the role of individual, prophetic thought, John Stackhouse writes:

> Christian communities do not escape the dynamics of group behaviour that may impede the Spirit's voice. Consider Paul, Francis, Luther, Kierkegaard, and others who spoke a shockingly alternative word to the dominant theology of their churches. ... Paul

---

11 From a quotation in a lecture give by Ben Myers on *'Rowan Williams Ecclesiology in the light of Easter.'*

provides for us an example of innovative dissent even within the early Christian community as he challenges the Jewish church with the legitimacy and success of the Gentile mission.[12]

And yet it remains true to say that we all need the help and correction that is derived from being part of a community. As a former Bishop of Bradford is reputed to have said:

> There is no way of belonging to Christ apart from belonging, gladly and irrevocably, to that ragbag of saints and fatheads, who go to make up the one, holy, catholic and apostolic church.

Second, as well as what the church *'shares in together'*, fellowship or *'koinonia'* refers to what the church *'shares out together'* - what is *given* as well as what is *received*. There is a big difference between being a congregation and being a community. A teenage girl reflecting on an experience of real community in her church wrote: 'Help me not to be okay just because everything is okay with *me*.' In community, if someone else is not okay, then to some degree, I am not okay.[13] Community has its own language in which the first person singular moves to the first person plural: from *I* to *we*.

In the little cameos of the church in the early chapters of Acts, the principle is stated twice:

> They would ... distribute the proceeds to all, as any had need'(Acts 2.45) and 'There was not a needy person among them, for as many as owned lands or houses sold them and brought the proceeds of what was sold. They laid it at the apostles' feet, and it was distributed to each as any had need (4.34-35).

Human need should always call forth compassion and service from the church, not as a 'bait and a bribe' to win people for Christ but simply because there are people in need and it is the right thing to do. Both ways of understanding the word *'koinonia'* make it clear that the Christian life is an 'other-person-centred' life.

---

12 John G. Stackhouse, *Need to Know*, (Oxford University Press, 2014), 184
13 Nancy Ortberg, *Looking for God*, (Tyndale House Publishers, 2008), 38

A worshipping community

They devoted themselves ... to the breaking of bread and to the prayers (Acts 2.42).

The repeated definite article - literally, '*the* breaking of the bread and *the* prayers' – suggests, on the one hand, a reference to the Eucharist (although at this stage as part of an '*Agape* meal'. This was an occasion on which the church gathered for a normal meal during which bread and wine was blessed and shared) and Liturgical prayers such as were used in the Temple courts (rather than private prayer). This early reference to Holy Communion is a reminder that the gift of faith does not come to us naked, unclothed, unaccompanied or un-sacramentalized.

To help his disciples to benefit from his impending death, Jesus did not give them a theory of the atonement. He gave them a meal. 'That meal' says Tom Wright, 'contains in itself not only all the various meanings of "atonement" that are worth considering, but also the means by which theories can be turned into real life. Personal, practical, political life. Kingdom-of-God-on-earth-as-in-heaven life.'[14]

Historically it is true to say that Catholics have stressed the sacraments and Protestants the Bible as the means of grace for Christian growth. Manifestly both views are one-sided. Why should we limp along on one leg when the good Lord has given us two? The gospel is made audible in words and visible in Sacraments. The great Reformer and compiler of the 1662 Anglican Prayer Book, Thomas Cranmer, claimed that in the sacraments the gospel is preached to our senses. He wrote:

For as the Word of God preached putteth Christ in our ears, so likewise these elements of water, bread, and wine, joined to God's Word, do after a sacramental manner put Christ into our eyes, mouths, hands, and all our senses.[15]

---

14 In an article published on the Fulcrum Web site, entitled, *'The cross and the Caricatures'*, Eastertide, 2007
15 Quoted in P. E. Hughes in *The Theology of the English Reformers*, (London, Hodder & Stoughton, 1965), 192

'In the long run,' as Michael Ramsey shrewdly commented, 'the Eucharist will be its own interpreter and teacher. For the supreme question is not what we make of the Eucharist, but what the Eucharist is making of us, as together with the Word of God it fashions us into the way of Christ'.[16]

It is clear from the glimpses of the early church's worship sketched by Luke that it was both *formal and informal*, for it took place both in the *temple courts* and in their *homes* (Acts 2.46). The informal 'house churches' or 'home fellowships' were intended to complement the more formal church services by encouraging friendships and mutual support. Today, what supplemented the local church has often evolved into being the church itself.

In addition, Stott points out that the worship of the early Christians was both *joyful and reverent*. They 'ate their food with glad and generous hearts' (Acts 2.46). On the day of Pentecost, the believers behaved in a manner that brought forth the accusation of drunkenness. Similarly, Paul anticipated that those who are indwelt by God's Spirit will manifest conduct comparable to that of the inebriated (Ephesians 5.18). The early Christians were a hilarious mob. At midnight, Paul and his companion Silas were in a prison in Philippi 'praying and singing hymns to God' while the other prisoners listened to them (Acts 16.25). This was no 'frothy, instant answer joy'. In the words of Karl Barth, it was a *'defiant, nevertheless joy'*. When they were under pressure, they *nevertheless* rejoiced. Even if their joy was often 'hilariously awful' it was still an infectious joy. Through their example, others were enabled to respond to whatever kind of hurricane hit them in praise rather than resentment. Following their example of joyful worship helped them to hear God's voice and grow in faith and understanding of God's purpose.

One of the worst things we can do in worship is to convey the impression that the Christian life is a sedate and dreary affair by disapproving of small children and tut-tutting whenever they make a noise, be it a happy

---

16 Quoted by Douglas Dales in *Glory: The Spiritual Theology of Michael Ramsey*, (Canterbury Press, 2003), 92

sound or otherwise. In his teaching, Jesus had much to say about little children. When his adult disciples attempted to shoo them aside, Jesus picked a child up in his arms, looked the disciples 'fair and square' in the eye and told them that rather than shooing them away, they should be chuffed to have them around. The attitude which says, 'you can't do that here' is all too common in churches and conveys a message of nervousness about God, rather than joy. I like the story told of a member of a Salvation Army band who was instructed by the band conductor to tone down his drum playing because he was drowning out the other musicians. He responded bluntly by saying, 'I am so happy I could bust the bloomin' drum'!

Nevertheless, the intoxicating joy of the early Christians was never irreverent. 'Awe came upon everyone' (Acts 2.43). The current trend in many churches is to turn worship into chic and slick 'Christotainment' as though the Christian assembly is a form of concert and the worship leader is a celebrity. Please, no hymns and Bach! In an age of entertainment, we have to be funny, likable and light to succeed. Michael Ramsey deplored the casual and unprepared way in which Anglicans of different stripes partake of Holy Communion. His words have proved prophetic:

> The awe in the individual's approach to Holy Communion, which characterised both the Tractarians and the Evangelicals of old, stands in contrast with the ease with which our congregations come tripping to the altar week by week.[17]

Ramsey warned that, 'the reception of communion is dreadful as well as precious.'[18] Communion costs. But Ramsey's words were not intended to diminish joy. He was a man who laughed a great deal and when he did, his whole bulk shook. He once remarked to a group of ordinands:

> Use your sense of humour. Laugh about things, laugh at the absurdities of life, laugh about yourself, and about your own absurdity. We are all of us infinitesimally small and ludicrous creatures within God's

17 Douglas Dales, *Glory: The Spiritual Theology of Michael Ramsey*, (Canterbury Press, 2003) 91
18 Ibid., 91

universe. You have to be serious, but never be solemn, because if you are solemn about anything there is a risk of becoming solemn about yourself.[19]

The combination of joy and awe, as of formality and informality, is a healthy balance in worship. Traditional forms of worship need not be side-lined by 'fresh expressions' if they are working well, as in many cathedrals today. The liturgy, music and ceremony evoke a sense of God's transcendence, God's shocking difference. Participating in this kind of formal worship is to have our expectations knocked sideways by the radiance and glory and beauty of God. In some places where conventional forms of worship continue to have attraction it will probably be best to continue them. In other places, unconventional forms will be needed in order to meet the needs of the community. This is what Rowan Williams meant by the need for the church of the future to become 'a mixed economy'.

A missionary community

Day by day the Lord added to their number those who were being saved (Acts 2.47b).

In many places in the Western world the church finds itself propagating the institution rather than propagating the gospel. Too much of what it does is of a trivial nature. It has settled down to maintaining the faith and making the occasional convert.

This is not to imply that the institutional life of the church is unimportant. The French diplomat Charles Maurice de Talleyrand once said: 'Without individuals nothing happens and without institutions nothing survives'. Those who are impatient with the institutional life of the church need to be helped to see that in the pages of the New Testament itself we find the apostle Paul, in collaboration with others, organizing, networking, tackling problems of authority, status, money and rival conceptions of the church. An institution is essentially an organized group that endures over time. Of course, the institution always stands in need of reform,

19 Michael Ramsey, *The Christian Priest Today*, (SPCK, 1972), 81

but forms and structures must be developed, if the church is to endure over time and space. We can hardly expect to find biblical support for diocesan managers, big budgets and high rise offices. Management structures have moved on from the days of the apostles. Nevertheless, there will always be a need for at least some minimal structure. With that caveat, it must still be admitted that many clergy and lay people today are frustrated by the amount of time spent on committees dealing with things that are not essential to furthering the gospel. We too easily lose sight of the fact that the Holy Spirit is a missionary Spirit. A Spirit-filled church will necessarily be a missionary church.

In both the Fourth Gospel (John 20.21f) and in Acts 2, the bestowal of the Spirit is closely linked with mission. To receive the Spirit means to be *'sent'* on Christ's mission. Sadly, there is truth in the statement that if the Holy Spirit was withdrawn from the early church, ninety percent of what it did would cease. By contrast, if the Holy Spirit was withdrawn from the church today, ninety percent of what it does would continue as usual.

The Iona Community, off the west coast of Scotland, has members all over the world and has established its own publishing house called *Wild Goose Publications*, named after the early Celtic symbol for the Holy Spirit. A wild goose is not an easy bird to control. When we speak of a 'Wild Goose Chase' we mean that we don't really know where we are going to end up.[20] Opening our lives to the Spirit of God can sometimes be like that. Jesus, in fact, used the image of the wind to make precisely that point. 'The wind blows where it chooses, and you will hear the sound of it, but you do not know where it comes from or where it goes' (John 3.8). Both symbols - wind and wild goose, leave us in no doubt that the wild Spirit of God cannot be domesticated or tamed. Life with the Spirit is always an exciting adventure. It is never dull. There is no one way of coming to faith. The church must beware of 'mono-method evangelism' and resist the temptation to parrot a formulaic gospel. God has his own secret stairway into every heart.

---

20 I have drawn on the image of the 'Wild Goose' as it was used in a sermon preached to the Synod of Gippsland by the much loved former bishop, the Rt Rev'd John McIntyre.

The great danger of organized churches – whether Catholic, Protestant or Pentecostal - is that they have often attempted to domesticate the Spirit of God. But as Jesus told Nicodemus, the wind blows where God chooses. The Protestant temptation is to relegate the Spirit's activity to the far-off apostolic days. The Bible is seen as the safest place for the Spirit. Those in the Catholic tradition have sometimes sought to domesticate the Spirit in the sacraments by putting her at the beck and call of the presiding priest or ordaining bishop.[21] And Pentecostalism has sometimes confined the Spirit to a two-staged initiation process consisting first of conversion and then of a subsequent 'baptism in the Spirit' authenticated by the gift of tongues. But the Spirit is sovereign and free and will not be domesticated. As Bishop John Taylor wrote, the Spirit is the 'surpriser-God', the 'unpredictable-God', the 'de-systematiser of systematic theologians'.[22]

Today, when we say '*in church*' it is hard to get some kind of a building out of our minds. Pete Ward has suggested that we need to be open to making a shift from seeing church as a gathering of people in one place at one time, that is, a congregation, to a notion of church as a series of relationships. He describes this as 'the shift from church as a *noun* to church as a *verb*'[23]. Instead of 'solid' church, this 'liquid' or 'fluid' view of the church allows it to flow along the networks in the community, bringing the message of Jesus into many and varied life situations. When we say that as Christians we are *'in Christ'* or *'in the body of Christ'* we are caught up in the liquid life of Christ. Membership is no longer measured by attendance in a congregation gathered in a building. Instead, it is assessed in terms of participation in a network. Pete Ward may well be right in suggesting that the future of the church is likely to be 'liquid' but if so, such churches will need to be self-consciously based on the gospel and the scriptures. Indeed, it seems to me, that the

---

21 Assuming that the groaning or sighs of the Spirit in Romans 8.26 refer to the groans of a woman in birth pain we are justified in using the feminine pronoun of the Spirit. Richard Bauckham has challenged this interpretation, arguing that the imagery derives not from the pangs of childbirth but from prophetic mourning and lamentation. See his discussion in *Bible And Ecology*, (DLT, 2010), 96
22 John V Taylor, *The Go-Between God*, (SCM, 1972)
23 Pete Ward, *Liquid Church*, (Paternoster, 2002), 2

more 'liquid' the church is in form, the more 'solid' must be its biblical and doctrinal basis. It is difficult to negotiate the tricky tension between being *culturally appropriate* and *culturally subversive*.

The book of Acts records God's Spirit using the preaching of the Apostles to effectively bring chaos to the early church. To imagine the apostle's staff meeting a day after Pentecost with several thousand new converts is to imagine a scene of total chaos! The growth of the Jerusalem church seems to have been phenomenal. The number of believers at the beginning of Acts is 120 (Acts 1.15). On the day of Pentecost 3,000 are added to the group (Acts 2.41) and after the response to Peter's preaching in Solomon's Porch the number is said to grow to 5,000 (Acts 4.4). By the time Paul visits Jerusalem two or three decades later 'many thousands of believers' are said to be there (Acts 21.17). Within two centuries Christianity was part of everyday life in most urban centres with bishops in positions of political power well before Constantine. The church needs to recover its nerve and talk about the good news *as* good news, not good advice.[24]

Mother Maria Skobtsova, a Russian nun who lived in Paris during the Second World War, has much to teach us about being open to the Holy Spirit. She was a member of the French Resistance and set up a 'convent' in a rented house where she assisted Jewish refugees and other needy people during the time of the Nazis. On Good Friday 1945 she was arrested by the Gestapo and ended her life in Ravensbruck Concentration camp when she took the place of a woman who was going to the Gas Chambers. She was an unconventional nun. After being divorced and a single mother, she took monastic vows and lived in a tiny community. Neighbours complained about the noisy parties she held in the convent late at night! She once said, 'Either Christianity is fire or there is no such thing'. She was right. The Spirit-filled person is a person with soul aflame.[25] It is too easy for Christians to drop into

---

24 Tom Wright, Simply Good News, 2015, HarperCollins, 125
25 The example of Mother Maria Skobtsova was drawn from a lecture given by Archbishop Rowan Williams, at a conference on *'The Holy Spirit in the World Today'* at Holy Trinity Brompton, London, May 20-21, 2010

a staid, soulless routine. It is a mistake which those who are filled with the effervescent life of the Spirit of God will not make.

Growth in numbers is not the only thing that matters in the mission of the church. When push comes to shove, it is always possible to get a thumping big crowd to turn up if the message promises some kind of reward, as in the brash health-and-wealth gospel. The same is so often true of the signs-and-wonders gospel or the psychological gospel of self-knowledge. In each case, the gospel is in danger of being presented as a commodity for a consumer culture. It has been wisely stated that 'all authentic evangelism should carry a health warning with its welcome'. Nevertheless, it is too easy to dismiss numerical growth, 'bums on pews' (so to speak), as an unworthy goal. We must not forget the church's 'backstory' in the Old Testament promise to Abraham, 'the divine conspiracy of blessing to the nations'.

At the corporate level, church communities must ask themselves 'what are the centres of vitality in our neighbourhood?' They will include schools, institutions involved in science and technology, health, welfare, Christianity and other religions. They will also ask 'what are the places of despair, weakness and disadvantage, sin and evil in our parish?' Mission means finding out what God is doing in our community and then joining in. It has been wisely suggested that people in the church might do well to stop worrying about what to say and concentrate instead on simply connecting, on striking up a relationship. Caring questions can open up the most amazing conversations and *conversation*, in the stories about Jesus, was often linked to *conversion*.

Such is Luke's ideal for the church. In the world of ideas and concepts it all sounds good and well. But the rubber hits the road when the *ideal* meets the *reality* of people's lives.

Rowan Williams himself has given wise advice in this regard. Here are some words to which I often need to return, sometimes in order to rebuke myself when I find I am becoming a crabby-old-man, sitting in the pews, criticizing under my breath! Williams' words bring me up short and help me to get back to a biblical understanding of what it means in practice to be part of God's church. He said:

When our church flourishes, praise God for his good gifts; when our church struggles and flounders, praise God for his faithfulness to us in our failure. And when, as so often, we see both together, we shall know that our heart must be with God who is greater than both human success and human failure, who is simply there, given to us for ever in Christ and his Spirit of promise.[26]

Questions for reflection

1. 'The overculture in which the churches now operate is so strong that unless there is robust and relevant teaching and preaching in our churches they will not survive the onslaught.' Do you think teaching should be a priority for the clergy?

2. 'Human need should always call forth compassion and service from the church, not as a 'bait and a bribe' to win people for Christ but simply because there are people in need and it is the right thing to do.' Discuss.

3. 'The awe in the individual's approach to Holy Communion which characterised both the Tractarians and the Evangelicals of old stands in contrast with the ease with which our congregations come tripping to the altar week by week.' Share how you personally prepare for Holy Communion.

4. 'Growth in numbers is not the only thing that matters in the mission of the church. Nevertheless, it is too easy to dismiss numerical growth, "bums on pews", as an unworthy goal.' Do you agree?

5. None of us gets the church on our own terms. The *reality* always falls short of the *ideal*. How do you cope with the imperfections of the church?

---

26 From a sermon marking the 1400th anniversary of the re-organisation of the Diocese of London, in St Paul's Cathedral on Saturday, 22nd May, 2004.

Prayer

A table that is round
It will take some sawing to be round-tabled,
Some redefining, some redesigning,
Some redoing and re-birthing of narrow-long churching.
Can be painful for people and tables!
It would mean no dais-ing and throning,
For but one King is there,
And he was a foot-washer
At table no less.
And what of narrow-long ministers
When they confront a round-table people,
After years of working up the table
To finally sit at its head,
Only to discover that the table
Has turned round?
They must be loved into roundness,
For God has called a people,
Not 'them' and 'us'.
'Them' and 'us' are unable to gather round
For at a roundtable there are no sides
And all are invited to wholeness and to food.
At one time our narrowing churches were built to resemble the cross
But it does no good for buildings to do so if lives do not.
Round-tabling means
No preferred seating,
No first and last, no better,
And no corners for 'the least of these'.
Round-tabling means being with, or part of, together and one.
It means room for the Spirit and gifts,
And disturbing profound peace for all.[27]

---

27 I am indebted to the Rev'd Dr Jonathan Inkpin for this brilliant piece. The author is unknown.

6. THE HOPE FOR A NEW CREATION

Professor Robert Jensen of the School of Journalism in the University of Texas at Austin was asked in an interview 'what gives you hope?' He replied:

> Nothing. I think hope is an illusion best abandoned. Our task is to see the world clearly, not wax poetic about hope.[1]

Like many today, Jensen has not understood the nature of biblical hope. It is not simply a matter of 'waxing poetic' - 'keeping your pecker up'. Nor is it a calculation of probabilities, like predicting the weather or Stock Exchange.

Dr Jim Packer distinguishes biblical hope from optimism in the following way:

> Optimism is a wish without a warrant; Christian hope is a certainty, guaranteed by God himself. Optimism reflects ignorance as to whether good things will ever actually come. Christian hope expresses knowledge that each day of his (sic) life, and every moment beyond it, the believer can say with truth, on the basis of God's own commitment, that the best is still to come.[2]

Hope, like a promise, cannot be verified. Its fulfilment lies in the future. But as Packer implies, how seriously we take the promise of a new creation depends on the character of whoever makes it. According to the Scriptures, the hope is not only based on the promise of Jesus but it is anticipated by his resurrection and is therefore utterly reliable. Christians are to be 'happy-hopers'. They are not *'wheelies'* who see history as cyclic, going round and round and getting nowhere. They are *'roadies'* who see history as an unfolding story that is going somewhere.

There are many aspects of the future consummation of history about which we must remain agnostic, particularly in regard to the manner of Christ's glorious appearance. When we think about it, questions

---

1 http://www.resilience.org/stories/2015-05-20/resilience-reflections-with-robert-jensen
2 J. I. Packer & Carolyn Nystrom, *Never Beyond Hope*, (IVP, 2000) 15

multiply. For instance, how can his appearance (*parousia*) be both personal and local and yet transcendent and universal? How can it occur simultaneously in Moscow and Melbourne? How can it be heralded with signs and yet be unexpected, like a thief breaking into a house? Here we are on the edge of mystery, trying to get our minds around something that is qualitatively new and wholly unprecedented. Because it lies in the future, it necessarily has to be spoken of in pictorial or figurative language. It is critical to keep in mind in reading books like the final book of the Bible, John of Patmos's Apocalypse, that *images are images are images*. John the visionary author speaks with reserve about the ineffable heavenly things he sees. He has to qualify everything he says with 'as it were' and 'the appearance of'. As Rowan Williams has said, 'this is language showing the weight it bears; the weight of a Word from outside ordinary categories'.[3] The priest and poet Studdert Kennedy makes this point in his poem entitled, 'Well?'

> There ain't no throne, and there ain't no books,
>> It's 'Im you've got to see,
> It's 'Im, just 'Im, that is the Judge
>> Of blokes like you and me.
> And, boys, I'd sooner frizzle up,
>> I' the flames of a burnin' 'Ell,
> Than stand and look into 'Is face,
>> And 'ear 'Is voice say--"*Well?*"[4]

Neither the scary, bizarre pictures of judgment nor the gold-bedecked streets of heaven are to be taken literally. Indeed it is impossible to do so, since fire and darkness exclude each other. Nor need we be petrified that our foreheads will someday be tattooed with the number 666. Biblical Christians need to distance themselves from the glibness and glee of the fundamentalist, science fiction approach to the preaching of heaven and hell. Richard Bauckham makes an important negative point in an article he wrote in the 1996 report of the Doctrine Commission of the Church of England. He said:

3 In a sermon to mark the Four Hundredth Anniversary of the 1611 Authorized Version of the Bible in Westminster Abbey, 16th November, 2011
4 G. A. Studdert Kennedy, *The Unutterable Beauty*, (Mowbray, 1983), 124

Hell is nothing more than not attaining salvation. It cannot be understood as something positive in itself. It only makes sense as a negative: not being saved. Salvation is not avoiding hell: rather hell is missing out on salvation. ... Hell is not an eternal chamber of horrors across the way from heaven. Hell is the fate of those who reject God's love. God's love cannot compel them to find their fulfilment in God, but there is no other way they can find fulfilment. They exclude themselves from the Source of all being and life.[5]

In a similar vein, Rowan Williams once referred to hell as being 'confronted unambiguously with love and not being able to look at it with joy'. In what follows we will consider the biblical hope in terms of the final trilogy – a new body; a new creation and a new relationship.

Re-embodiment

At the consummation of the kingdom of God, the tension between 'the now and the not yet' will be relieved by the re-embodiment of resurrection after the disembodiment of death. In this present life humans are always vulnerable to accident and disease. Our bodies and minds are as fragile as egg shells. When we are sick and in need, we can plead to God for healing. But we cannot presume upon it. Paul prayed repeatedly for the removal of a 'thorn from his flesh.' He gives us the summary of a wrestling match he had with God over its removal when he prayed: 'three times I pleaded with the Lord to take it away from me' (2 Corinthians 12.8). Physical healing in this life depends on God's sovereign pleasure. Tom Smail has pointed out that to the person who believes today but has not seen the answer come today, there comes the call to hope. He says:

> God is not by any means confined to today, as if when it is over all God's possibilities are over with it. God is free to act tomorrow, and at any time he chooses in all the series of tomorrows, and beyond that in the Great Tomorrow when the whole inheritance is at last delivered and the sons and daughters of God at last come into their own.[6]

---

5 Richard Bauckham, First Published in *News Extra*.
6 Thomas A.Smail, *The Forgotten Father*, (Hodder & Stoughton, 1980), 142

The final answer to the healing question will be the glorified resurrection body. Writing to the Philippians Paul says,

> But our citizenship is in heaven, and it is from there that we are expecting a Saviour, the Lord Jesus Christ. He will transform the body of our humiliation that it may be conformed to the body of his glory, by the power that also enables him to make all things subject to himself (Phil. 3:20-21).

In this passage Paul claims that Jesus' resurrection body is a paradigm of the resurrection body that will be given to all believers. 'God doesn't create Jesus version 2, from scratch'. That would be a rejection of creation. 'God re-creates Jesus from his very own dead bones'. And what God did to the atoms and molecules of the body of Jesus that explosive 'third' day is what He intends to do on the 'final' day for all who place their trust in him. However we must be careful not to convey the impression of a crude physical continuity between our earthly bodies and the new resurrection bodies. The new resurrection body cannot depend simply on the continuity of matter. Even in this life we know that the matter of which our bodies are composed is completely replaced every seven years. In employing the metaphor of the resurrection body as 'a building from God, a house not made with hands, eternal in the heavens', Paul is seeking to guard against too crude an idea of continuity (2 Corinthians 5.1). The continuity of bodily identity does not depend on continuity of matter.

On the other hand, it has often been mistakenly thought that when Paul wrote about a 'spiritual' resurrection body, he meant a 'non-material' body, like a ghost (1Cor. 15:44). This is a hope which contradicts what it means to be human. It looks to a future ethereal other-world where we become mere disembodied spirits. Tom Wright has pointed out that the Greek adjective 'spiritual' is used to describe not what the resurrection body is made of, but what or who is animating it. The risen Jesus had a physical body animated by God's life-giving Spirit. This is a hope which has implications not only for our body but for our whole being. Paul finishes his first letter to the Thessalonians with a reassuring prayer:

6. The Hope for a New Creation

May your whole spirit, soul and body be kept blameless at the coming of our Lord Jesus Christ (1 Thessalonians 5:23).

As we age, many of us begin to suffer loss of memory. But the final resurrection gives assurance that nothing of value will be lost. All that God treasures will be gathered into the new and eternal creation. Alzheimer's sufferers will, in the resurrection, be who they were in the whole of their mortal life, not merely who they were in their dementia at the point of death. The whole of what has happened in this transient life, will be gathered up, healed and transfigured into eternal life and eternal time.

Christianity differs from the dualistic ideas that find expression in Eastern religions such as Hinduism and Buddhism, where the body is regarded as an encumbrance in which we are imprisoned and from which we must eventually escape. Such views are also evident in some forms of New Age teaching which maintain that we go through many cycles of reincarnation, returning again and again to new bodies in this world. This process is one of self-salvation. By good works and enlightenment we may eventually escape bondage to our earthly bodies and be absorbed into Nirvana.

In contrast, the Christian hope is not one of reincarnation but resurrection. It is this future transformation of the whole person, body included, which addresses the pervasive fear of a personal loss of freedom in growing old. The New Testament doesn't cover up the probable losses we face in the ageing process. On the contrary, the risen Christ tells the apostle Peter:

Very truly, I tell you, when you were younger, you used to fasten your belt and to go wherever you wished. But when you grow old, you will stretch out your hands, and someone else will fasten a belt around you and take you where you do not wish to go (John 21.18).

Like Peter, many of us, as we grow old, will end our days with a loss of individual freedom, and a sense of 'being taken where we did not wish to go'. But alongside of the undeniable fact of growing old and moving from a past of living in the direction of a coming death, we who are united with Christ are also moving from a past of death in the direction of coming life. Paul speaks of this reverse direction of growing when he tells the Ephesians that they are to 'grow up in every way into him who is the head, into Christ' (Ephesians 4.15). This is surely the best news anyone could hear.

One of my brothers, Allan, was involved in an accident which left his spinal cord badly damaged. He is now severely paralysed, unable to dress himself or feed himself and totally dependent for most of the ordinary daily routine functions on others. When I think of him now living in an Aged Care facility, I take encouragement from some words of Joni Eareckson Tada. In 1967 aged seventeen, she was injured in a diving accident when she misjudged the depth of the water. Ever since that fatal day, she has been a quadriplegic, paralysed from the neck down. While she was still trying to come to terms with this horrible accident, she would go to her Episcopal church in a wheelchair. The problem with being in the wheelchair, she found, was that at a certain point in her church's liturgy every Sunday, the priest called everyone to kneel – which drove home to her the fact that she was stuck in a wheelchair.

'With everyone kneeling, I certainly stood out. And I couldn't stop the tears', she said. But it wasn't because of self-pity. She went on to say: 'Sitting there, I was reminded that in heaven I will be free to jump up, dance, kick, and do aerobics. And … sometime before the guests are called to the banquet table at the Wedding Feast of the Lamb, the first thing I plan to do on resurrected legs is to drop on grateful, glorified knees. I will quietly kneel at the feet of Jesus … can you imagine the hope that the resurrection gives someone who is spinal cord-injured like me?[7]

We all have aches and pains that pester and annoy. For some, such experiences are fleeting and momentary. For others, they are chronic and lifelong. In the eventide of my life I appreciate more fully the wit and wisdom of C. S. Lewis in some words he wrote to an elderly friend:

---

7 Joni Eareckson Tada, *Heaven Your Real Home*, (Zondervan, 2001), 53

As we grow older, we become like old cars – more and more repairs and replacements are necessary. We must look forward to the fine new machines (latest Resurrection model) which are waiting for us, we hope, in the Divine garage![8]

Paul points out that the wonder of the Resurrection model is 'far more than the old repaired: it is one recreated in Christ, not a last-minute fix but as God's from eternity – a people "predestined, called, justified, glorified"' (Romans 8.30).[9]

Renovation

The Swiss Roman Catholic theologian, Hans Kung spoke of the consummation of the Kingdom of God as 'creation healed'. It is beyond our comprehension what such a transformation of creation might be like but it is reassuring to know that God is not simply going to write off the world which he has so intricately created. The most precious things on earth will continue. There's a lovely story (probably one that has grown in the telling) told about the sixteenth century Reformer Martin Luther looking up from his desk as he was writing on Romans chapter 8 about the future glory for which the whole creation groans. Out of the corner of his eye he saw his faithful dog in the corner of the room. Patting him on the head he said: 'And you will have a little golden tail!' But the future healing and renovation of creation will not be for the nice parts of nature only. It will involve the whole creation including the dark chaotic forces and untamed energies in the world – even the annoying mosquito in the nudist camp who complained, 'So much to do that it is impossible to know where to begin!' Somehow, our reconciliation with God and one-another, will spill over into the reconciliation and the transfiguration of the whole creation. Our liberation involves the liberation of the entire animate and inanimate creation. C.S. Lewis describes heaven as being more solid, more real than our present world. This is a healthy corrective to our tendency to assume that what we experience now is the only solid reality.

8 C. S. Lewis, *Letters to an American Lady*, (Eerdmans, 2014), 78
9 Charles Sherlock, *The Words and The Word*, (Mosaic Press, 2013), 159

As mentioned above, Paul speaks in poetic terms of the believer's yearning for such a renovated cosmos in Romans 8:

> I consider that the sufferings of this present time are not worth comparing with the glory about to be revealed to us. For the creation waits with eager longing for the revealing of the children of God; for the creation was subjected to futility, not of its own will but by the will of the one who subjected it, in hope that the creation itself will be set free from its bondage to decay and will obtain the freedom of the glory of the children of God. We know that the whole creation has been groaning in labour pains until now; and not only the creation, but we ourselves, who have the first fruits of the Spirit, groan inwardly while we wait for adoption, the redemption of our bodies. For in hope we were saved. Now hope that is seen is not hope. For who hopes for what is seen? But if we hope for what we do not see, we wait for it with patience (Romans 8:18-25).

Tom Wright has become one of the leading and most persuasive Christian exponents of this future hope for a sick creation. He argues that God will do for the whole creation, animate and inanimate, what he did for Jesus at Easter. He suggests that this vision of the future in Romans chapter 8 is so big and so dazzling, that most Christians read about it and then blink their eyes, and hurry on to the more 'personal' application of the passage. Too often, clergy have thought of ministry in the church in terms of saving individual souls for a disembodied heaven or as Wright likes to say, 'saving souls rather than saving wholes.' Richard Bauckham agrees and says:

> The Christian hope has constantly been understood as hope for human fulfilment in another world ('heaven') rather than as a hope for the eternal future of this world in which we live.[10]

As we have already seen, the hope held out to believers in the New Testament is not an individualistic, moralistic vision of personal salvation, in which we are air-lifted out of the ante-chamber of the present created order with all its problems into a non-historical world.

---

10 Richard Bauckham & Trevor Hart, *Hope Against Hope*, (DLT, 1999), 129

The Australian theologian Simon Holt humorously describes the way in which eschatology (the study of the last things) has become for many people a form of 'escape-ology'. He writes,

> I saw a bumper sticker on a car a few weeks back. At the time the driver was attempting a dangerous and illegal u-turn directly in front of me. Now in bold print, the sticker read, 'I'm Heaven-bound! This world is not my home.' Given his driving, I thought at the time that the truth of this statement was probably more imminent than he realised. Later, as I pondered the declaration, I realised just how powerful it is as a theological statement, and how much it reflects a theology that ignores the neighbourhood. It is true that in some parts of the evangelical church we are much more preoccupied with where we are going than where we are. The dominant motivation for mission is bound up in the anticipation of eternity in heaven and concurrently, the desire to rescue those bound for hell.[11]

The bugbear for Wright, Bauckham and Holt, is the suggestion that Jesus helps us go to heaven rather than brings heaven to earth. If God's creation simply amounts to a throw-away world destined to perish and all that matters is the saving of individual souls, we are left with no real motivation for creation-care. But if the new creation involves the transformation of the present creation and not its replacement, care of the environment becomes an important element in Christian mission. Personal evangelism is vital. But God changes people in order to change the communities of which they are a part. Nor should our concern stop with the local community. It must go on to involve responsibility in the wider community of the planet.

The Bible anchors hope for the future of creation in the promises of God. Wealthy Western Countries, such as Australia, are now sitting on a fault-line between local good order and the huge demands of a wider, global community for comprehensive, distributive justice. Refugees fleeing the regime changes in Syria, Libya and Iraq are bringing suffering on levels not seen since 1945. An economic hurricane is

11 Simon Carey Holt, *God Next Door*, (Acorn Press, 2007), 84

gathering strength. Many find it to be an uncomfortable place. Few, if any can see the route back to security and stability. It is as if the whole world is being shaken. The writer of the letter to the Hebrews speaks of the 'removal of what is shaken – that is, created things – so that what cannot be shaken may remain' (Hebrews 12.27). Faced not only with outrageous cruelty and violence but also global ecological catastrophe, the sobering words of Richard Bauckham are worth weighing carefully. He writes with the global ecological catastrophe in mind but his words are applicable to a wide range of present global problems:

> When I think about the future of the Christian church in our western society, it seems to me very bleak in the short-term. I think the church is virtually bound to become an increasingly marginalized minority in a deeply hostile culture, and I doubt whether the church is really prepared for that role. When I think about the future of the world, I tend to even greater pessimism. I do not see how it is possible for the world to make the kind of radical changes that alone will avert global ecological catastrophe. I know I may be wrong about these things. But the point I want to make is that Christian hope is something else: not a calculation of probabilities, not a temperamental inclination to look on the bright side, but trusting God's promises that, in spite of and beyond the worst that may happen, God will fulfil his purposes for his world. This is hoping against hope, as we say. It is hope that has no basis other than God, which is to say it has the only basis that can in the end be reliable[12].

Bauckham's words may not be popular in religious circles where it is fashionable to be uncertain and hesitant. Admittedly, when it comes to the future some Christians are far too dogmatic. Fundamentalist evangelists often give the impression that the Bible was written to give inside esoteric information about the end-times. They devise flowcharts of the sequence of events that will precede the final consummation of the world. But Jesus himself admitted to being ignorant as to when this will occur. His followers must therefore be prepared to be agnostic

---

12 See further on this theme, Richard Bauckham & Trevor Hart, *Hope Against Hope*, (DLT, 1999).

about many aspects of the end-time. There are many uncertainties. We must not go beyond what God has revealed. But in addition to uncertainties there are certainties. God is faithful. God can be trusted and it is confidence in his promises that drives us in the present with a strong desire to take responsible action for the well-being of the planet.

Several years ago, after an early morning swim in the Newcastle sea baths, I was sitting on a public seat, eating a bowl of muesli and looking out at the ships queued up to come into the port. As I sat on that bench seat savouring the beauty of the seascape and delighting in the dolphins cavorting, playing and splashing, the creation became for me what John Calvin called, 'the theatre of God's glory'. I felt as if I was in the presence of unutterable 'wonder-fulness', an attender at one of God's many shows that give clues to his goodness. Unlike humans, the non-human creation glorifies God simply by being itself, as God made it. The dolphins were doing what God made them to do. They seemed to be having such fun. I was awestruck. I wanted to pull out all stops and sing the Hallelujah Chorus, 'King of Kings and Lord of Lords'. An old lady, out on her morning walk, paused in front of me and said: 'You wouldn't be dead for quids would you!' She summed up my feelings exactly. Her words matched the old saying that: 'Life is not measured by the number of breaths we take, but by the moments that take our breath away'. The creation exists to elicit joy and to direct it back to God in praise. There are surely moments for all of us when we intuitively feel that creation, whether in the form of a breathtaking sunrise or sunset or a new born babe, though not a knock-out proof for God's existence, is nonetheless a powerful indicator of a divine Creator. These are occasions when we run out of adjectives. I was speechless. In reflective silence I gave thanks to the Creator.

But there is a flip side to this story. Our world is achingly beautiful but also awesomely ugly. My joy and delight were blighted by an intruding thought. The nine ships silhouetted against the brilliant morning sky and queued up to come into Newcastle port, were a worrying omen of what humans were doing to muffle the praise of the dolphins. Newcastle is the biggest port for exporting coal in the world. Although the *value* of coal has fallen in recent times, the *volume* of coal being exported to China and elsewhere shows no sign of abating. The addiction of wealthy nations to fossil fuel is one of the major causes of the tragedy of the greenhouse effect that has irreversibly changed the atmosphere and the oceans. Climate change has been rightly described as a 'weapon of mass destruction'.[13] It is vital that the coal stays where it is, namely, 'down under' (meaning, in Australia) and 'down under' (meaning, beneath the ground). As a result of our botched efforts, creation cannot now sing God's praise as fully as it was created to do. As I drank in the combination of the beauty of that morning and the worrying sign of the coal ships on the horizon, I turned my fearful thoughts to the sublime vision painted by the psalmists of what life will be like after the 'Divine Cleanup of the World'.[14] Humans will join with all God's creatures as partners in praise in singing 'a new song' in 'a new creation':

> O sing to the Lord a new song;
> sing to the Lord, all the earth.
> Let the heavens be glad, and let the earth rejoice;
> let the sea roar, and all that fills it;
> let the field exult, and everything in it.
> Then shall all the trees of the forest sing for joy
> before the Lord; for he is coming, for he is coming to judge the earth.
> He will judge the world with righteousness,
> And the peoples with his truth (Psalm 96.1,11-13).

Someone has speculated that at the last judgement, God will ask a single question: 'Did you enjoy my creation?' As we join the party that God will put on for our homecoming, we will be able to respond in the way of St Augustine: 'All our activity will be "Amen" and "Alleluia"'.[15]

---

13 Words echoed by Hans Blix, the former UN weapons inspector.
14 John Dominic Crossan's phrase in *How To Read The Bible & Still Be A Christian*, (HarperCollins, 2015), 9
15 Quoted in Richard Bauckham & Trevor Hart, *Hope Against Hope*, (DLT, 1999), 156

Reunion

In the last section I referred to the emphasis that Tom Wright has given to the cosmic scope of the 'good news'. Creation has a future. Though this is a much needed correction to a gospel message that focuses exclusively on individual salvation, Peter Orr, a lecture in New Testament at Moore College Sydney, has issued an important rider to Wright's emphasis when he says:

> Earlier generations of Evangelicals may have unhelpfully denied the goodness of creation. But the solution is not to overcorrect the error. The New Testament affirms creation, but it doesn't exalt creation. Often modern reflection on eschatology and the idea of the continuity of creation and new creation ends in exalting creation. The New Testament affirms creation but it exalts Christ. So our activity is not primarily to be done in view of the fact that there will be a new creation, but that one day Christ will be seen for who he is. Thinking about the impact of the resurrection on the Christian life must go hand in hand with looking at the application that the New Testament itself makes.[16]

Orr draws attention to where our faith should be focussed. In the final book of the Bible, the book of Revelation, Jesus Christ says: 'I am the *Alpha* and the *Omega*, the *first* and the *last*, the *beginning* and the *end*' (22.13). The historical human Jesus, shares the divine identity of the one God who also declares himself to be 'the First and the Last' (Isaiah 41.4; 44.6). The Messiah, Jesus, is the *origin* and *goal* of the whole of history. Biblical history is essentially a Christological meta-narrative. The key to the whole of the 'big story' we have been considering is Jesus' own story.

Anticipating this glory is something Paul encourages his readers to do when he writes: 'I consider that the sufferings of this present time are not worth comparing with the glory about to be revealed to us' (Romans 8.18). Our present troubles are trivial, ephemeral flea-bites in comparison with the tons of glory that await us. Creation's destiny

---

16 Peter Orr, The Briefing, September, 2014

is intertwined with that of God's children who wait for their adoption and the embrace of their glorified Lord. That prospect, Paul says, ought to fill the believer with hope and longing. In a similar vein, writing towards the end of his life, Paul encourages his young co-worker and companion, Timothy: 'From now on there is reserved for me the crown of righteousness, which the Lord, the righteous judge, will give me on that day, and not only to me but also to all who have longed for his appearing'(2Timothy 4.8). Paul was not alone in living with this joyous anticipation. In his first letter, John spells out the prospect of the *vision of God* which is actually the *vision of the glorified Christ*: 'Beloved, we are God's children now; what we will be has not yet been revealed. What we do know is this: when he is revealed, we will be like him, for we will see him as he is' (1 John 3.2).

The Bible however does not teach that every individual will ultimately be saved and enjoy the beatific vision of the exalted Christ. Such a belief, known as the doctrine of universal salvation or 'universalism' is held by many people, often for emotional rather than intellectual reasons. Anyone who has not felt deeply the attraction of universalism can scarcely have been moved by the wonder of God's love. But the terrifying fact is that God's love will never overrule human freedom. There is no power that can force the human heart. God will not take us by the scruff of the neck and say, 'You will believe'. Because God loves us, he will not interfere with our freedom. Love is at the heart of the Christian message and we must never tire of saying so.

The German theologian and pastor, Helmut Thielicke makes this point with a powerful pastoral story. He tells how he received a letter from a mother anxious about the eternal destiny of her 18 year old son who was killed in World War 11. Thielicke replied that he had no means of knowing whether God had received the boy into heaven, and for the sake of truth could not offer false assurances. But, he continued, Scripture says, 'Cast all your anxieties on him, for he cares for you' (1Peter 4.6). 'The question of your son's destiny is an anxiety for you. So cast it on God! We have the promise that we never cast amiss, but that our anxiety always "hits home" to him'. This is not an 'answer', but a redirection of the questioner to a place where she can find peace even though her question remains unanswered. However burning the question may be, to know the answer is ultimately less important than to know God and God's care.[17] We cannot be blandly confident about who is going where. The Bible does not give us all the answers, but it does show us the character of God, and we can trust God's judgments because we can trust him. We can affirm Abraham's question, 'Shall not the Judge of all the earth do what is just?' (Genesis 18.25).

I'm not sure if I'm typical or unusual but whereas in the past thoughts about death were few and far between, now, in the eventide of my life, I find myself slipping more frequently into thoughts that anticipate my final hours on this earth. Even as I write these final paragraphs, I have clocked up another year. If I am honest, the inevitability and manner of my dying evokes a kaleidoscope of responses within me, extending from denial and fear to resigned acceptance. It's not the dying that's the issue: it's living until I die. I must admit to a sneaking sympathy with the sentiments of Mark Twain when he said: 'Life would be infinitely happier if we could be born at the age of eighty and gradually approach the age of eighteen'.

But old age doesn't have to be a grim affair of shrinking horizons. As we grow older we are confronted with a choice: to live in the past and grow resentful at what we have lost; or to live now, accepting the inevitable loss of energy and recurrent weariness, but feeding off happy memories with thankfulness for all that has been. So much depends on our attitude. The reality is that finding joyful hope sometimes requires discipline and determination. There is nothing surprising in this. Each of us is subject to mood swings. We should never disguise or deny our true feelings. But neither should we necessarily embrace them as the truth. They can be a powerful illusion. We must regularly remind ourselves of the truth that Jesus remains risen and the source of hope. We may sometimes require help and support in reconnecting with that hope. That, in part, is why

---

17 Helmut Thielicke, *Between Heaven and Earth* (James Clarke, 1967), 109

church membership and Christian friendship are so important. As a preacher myself, I have good reason to take seriously the words of Richard Baxter (1615 – 91), one of the much maligned and misunderstood Puritan theologians, who said, 'It is a great part of a Christian's skill and duty, to be a good preacher to himself (*sic*) ... Two or three sermons a week from others is a fair proportion; but two or three sermons a day from thyself, is ordinarily too little.'[18] Baxter disciplined himself in a form of meditation that consisted in bringing the promises of God's future to mind and having reflected on them by way of discursive thought he aroused his affections of love, desire, hope, courage and joy by means of soliloquy (that is, preaching to himself in the presence of God).

It is the world of God's future that we also touch and taste by sharing in the Eucharist, which is the sacrament of a new world born out of the travail of costly love. As a foretaste of the heavenly banquet, a taste of heaven on earth, the Eucharist turns us into 'praiseaholics'. In his accounts of the meal, St Paul claims that every time Christians meet around bread and wine, they 'proclaim the Lord's death until he comes' (1 Corinthians 11.26). In heaven, we will enjoy God for God's sake. And if that is how we are to spend eternity, we ought to start getting accustomed to it now. Heaven begins now. Echoing the joyous choral liturgy in heaven, we join in singing 'with angels and archangels, and with the whole company of heaven'[19]: 'Holy, holy, holy, the Lord God the Almighty, who was and is and is to come'. So next Sunday, as you stand or kneel to sing the three-fold *sanctus*, do it with gusto!

There was no geriatric self-pity in St Paul. Physical infirmity was a nuisance admittedly. But it was no cause for despair. He tells us:

> We do not lose heart. Though outwardly we are wasting away, yet inwardly we are being renewed day by day (2 Corinthians 4.16).

Paul's phrase 'we do not lose heart' meant a lot to the great English Evangelical preacher, John Stott.[20] Towards the end of his life he lived

---

18 Richard Baxter, *Practical Works*, (23 vol; ed. W. Orme; 1830), 2.392
19 A Prayer Book for Australia, The Holy Communion, Second Order, Thanksgiving 1, 128
20 See for example chapter 1 in his book, *Challenges of Christian Leadership*, (IVP, 2014), 17

in a community for retired clergy in Surrey. On one occasion a visiting friend asked whether he was happy. His response was that while he would not say he was happy, he could say that he was content, citing Paul's words: 'I am not saying this because I am in need, for I have learned to be content whatever the circumstances' (Philippians 4.11). Throughout his life, Stott had learnt to trust in the providential care of God, through which alone comes contentment. He exemplified the title of Billy Graham's book: *Nearing Home: Life, Faith and Finishing Well*. It is a title which captures the touching words of the song sung by the old man Simeon as he took the Christ child in his arms and blessed him (Luke 2.29-32). It is known to generations of Anglicans by the Latin of its opening words, *Nunc Dimittis*: *'Now, Lord, you let your servant go in peace: your word has been fulfilled'*. Its appropriateness for Evening worship is that it expresses a readiness for death, 'of which every night brings a type of sleep'. Simeon had been told that he would not die until he had seen the Lord's Christ. But now that he had seen Jesus, he was quite ready to die, for he recognized him as God's salvation. He knew that his time of waiting was over.

In my *'finishing'* years, I am determined not to fritter away my time on trivia. Without playing down present responsibilities, I try to put aside dithering doubts about the trilogy of hope that lies beyond this life: *'reunion'* with Christ, my parents and other loved ones (as well as meeting up with Saint Paul to discuss the meaning of what he wrote in Romans chapters 9, 10 and 11!); a *'renovated and renewed creation'* that has been taken beyond destructive behaviour, disease, death, decay and decomposition; and a *'new resurrection body'* without an annoying bladder or any other aches and pains! In the words of St Paul, 'I do not consider that I have made it my own; but this one thing I do: forgetting what lies behind and straining forward to what lies ahead, I press on toward the goal for the prize of the heavenly call of God in Christ Jesus (Philippians 3.13,14).

The morning, described earlier in this chapter, when I sat beside the sea in Newcastle watching the dolphins splashing and playing, I didn't want it to come to an end. But it did. There was yet another damn diocesan meeting to attend! Thank God, heaven will be different. In the words of the anonymous writer who added a final verse to John Newton's well known hymn, *Amazing Grace*:

> When we've been there ten thousand years,
> Bright shining as the sun,
> We've no less days to sing God's praise
> Than when we first begun.

With what has been called 'prospective nostalgia' I imagine that heaven will be an experience of sheer unadulterated joy. If this is true, as I believe it is, the question that I must ask myself is: 'am I now living my way into the kind of relationship with God which will make heaven a joy?' Even just a peek into God's future ought to prompt me to cry out, if not in the Aramaic of the early Christian prayer - 'Maranatha' (Come Lord Jesus) then at least in my colloquial Aussie jargon - 'Bring it on.'

Questions for reflection

1. What human emotions does the thought of death evoke in you? Do you find Jim Packer's distinction between biblical hope and optimism helpful?

2. In what way does Paul's account of the re-embodied Jesus in 1 Corinthians 15 help you in your thinking about the nature of heaven?

3. Christians are often portrayed as those who miss out on the pleasures of life, because, it is falsely claimed that God doesn't want us to enjoy ourselves too much. But God is not mean or stingy in his blessings. Share about an occasion when you have delighted and revelled in the pleasures of God's creation.

4. How helpful do you find Richard Bauckham's words about hell: 'It only makes sense as a negative: not being saved.' Do you think much about heaven or do you see it as a distraction from living now?

5. For what reasons do people find Universalism attractive?

A Litany of Praise[21]

To the source of all love in the Father. **Amen!**

To the self-gift of love in the Son. **Amen!**

To the boundless mercy of love in the cross. **Amen!**

To the victory of love in the resurrection. **Amen!**

To the Spirit of love breathing through all time and space. **Amen!**

To the celebration of such love in the church. **Amen!**

To the glory of love in the life of the world to come. **Amen!**

---

21 Anthony J. Kelly, *God Is Love*, (Liturgical Press, 2012), 116

APPENDIX A: THE BIBLICAL TEMPLE-MOTIF

This ancient notion of the temple as 'sacred space' is a major theme that runs throughout the biblical narrative from creation to new creation. The tabernacle carried around as the dwelling place of God during the wilderness wanderings was the forerunner to the temple built in Solomon's reign. Israel's rebellion led to God's presence leaving the temple. The temple was destroyed by the Babylonians in 587 BCE (Ezekiel 10). After seventy years of exile in Babylon a remnant of the people returned to Jerusalem and the temple was rebuilt. Those who could remember the former temple were greatly disappointed, leading to further prophetic promises, widening the vista to universal dimensions. God's presence was made known according to Matthew's Gospel as *'Emmanuel – God with us'* (Matthew 1.23) and according to John's Gospel, Jesus in his humanity, is the temple presence of the God of Israel (John 1.14).

All four Gospels mention that Jesus cleansed the Temple by driving out the money makers and the money changers. But John transposes this narrative from the end of Jesus ministry to the beginning. By this change of location, John shows more clearly than the other three Gospels that Jesus had come to replace the temple. True worship is now centred, not in a building, but in the person of Jesus: 'Destroy this temple, and in three days I will raise it up … but he was speaking of the *temple of his body'*. This is an important theme in John's Gospel. Jesus replaces Jewish institutions such as the Temple and the Jewish feasts.

John is unveiling for his readers what we might call his *'Temple Christology'*. And for John, Jesus is not only the Temple in person, he is the one in whom everything that would normally happen in the Temple is fulfilled. He is the *great High Priest* (and in Chapter 17 we read the so-called *High Priestly Prayer* when Jesus prays for his disciples and the future Church). All the functions of the Temple – festival, presence, priesthood, and sacrifice – have devolved onto Jesus. This is the heart of John's 'high Christology'.

In his letters to the Christians in Corinth, Paul applies temple imagery to Christians in whom God now dwells by means of the Holy Spirit, both individually (1 Corinthians 6.19) and corporately (1 Corinthians 3.16). Finally, the Biblical narrative looks to the future when, as C. S. Lewis puts it, 'the anaesthetic fog which we call "nature" or "the real world" fades away and the Presence in which you have always stood becomes palpable, immediate and unavoidable'.[1] There will be no more temple because the 'temple is the Lord God the Almighty and the Lamb' (Revelation 21.22).

---

1 C. S. Lewis, *Mere Christianity*, (Fount Paperbacks, 1997),179

APPENDIX B: HISTORICAL TRUTHFULNESS

I can only just dip my toe in the water here. Inadequate as they are, a few brief comments on this important question may be helpful. Some Bible scholars are historical maximalists with an obsession for historical accuracy; while others are historical minimalists for whom all that really matters is that the Bible is a good story.

Historical maximalists

Extreme historical maximalists are those who are committed to believing that all the stories recounted in the Bible are historically and factually true in every detail, even the story of Jonah. Someone has jokingly suggested that such people would consider that the Garden of Eden story 'would be enhanced by the discovery of a fossilized apple with a couple of bites taken from it!' Less extreme Old Testament conservative scholars, such as those who belong to the so-called 'Albright school', are interested in the discoveries of archaeology, not in order to prove the historical truthfulness of the stories but to illustrate their plausibility. This is done by comparing, for example, the similar customs of adoption, inheritance and marriage in the stories of Abraham, Isaac and Jacob, with those discovered in ancient texts from the second millennium, such as those that have been found in the famous Nuzi texts. In addition, the semi-nomadic life of Abraham's clan fits perfectly into the cultural and political milieu of mass migration in the early second millennium. However, when we recall that these early patriarchs spent most of their life travelling through hundreds of kilometres of desert country we may consider that it is not surprising that archaeological digs have come up with little evidence that is able to prove or disprove the existence of Abraham.

Historical minimalists

For historical minimalists, such as Neils Peter Lemche, the whole sweep of the Old Testament narrative from Adam to Ezra and Nehemiah contains very little actual history.[1] Most of it is complete fiction. Any

---

1 See for example, Neils Peter Lemche, *The Old Testament – between Theology and History, A Critical Survey.*

correlation between the Biblical record and extra-Biblical evidence is regarded as incidental. The ancient authors, just like contemporary authors of historical fiction, tried to ensure that their stories were set in a relatively realistic and accurate setting.

David Tacey is another who has joined the *historyless* chorus. Tacey's interest is primarily in the ideas of the faith, not in any of the events described, which he claims are an amalgam of myth and history. Myth has been defined by Thomas Mann as 'a story about the way things never were, but always are' – that is, it's about the way things never were in that it's not about something that happened. That's not its point. But it's about the way things always are. That is what makes it a true myth as distinct from a false myth.[2]

Tacey suggests that that the literary form of the biblical text is more akin to poetry than prose and, if the churches don't wake up to this fact, they will implode. He says:

> The challenge facing religions is to overcome naïve belief while not falling into a slump of despair once we realize that what we have been taught as facts are metaphors.[3]

For Lemche, Tacey and many others, the Biblical narrative is a collection of stories wrapped around a remarkably thin framework of historical facts. They support their case by pointing to the lack of documents, inscriptions and archaeological items that have survived from the different periods covered in the Old Testament metanarrative. But as John Dickson has pointed out, such discoveries are 'entirely hit-and-miss and woefully incomplete.' Dickson frankly admits that:

> We don't have even 1 percent of the records of the New Kingdom (the period in which the pivotal event of the Exodus from Egypt is thought to have occurred). And with more than 99 percent of the evidence missing, who can say for sure what did *not* happen?[4]

---

2 Quoted in Marcus J. Borg, *Putting Away Childish Things*, (HarperOne, 2010), 160
3 David Tacey, *Beyond literal Belief: Religion as Metaphor*, (Garratt, 2015), 13
4 John Dickson, *A Doubter's Guide To The Bible*, (Zondervan, 2014), 71

Moreover, this historical minimalist position is based on the assumption that the biblical record itself is not evidence. Scholars such as Lemche assume that it is possible to describe the religious beliefs of the Biblical writers neutrally and objectively. On balance, it seems that the books of the Bible can only work as 'good news' if the key events described actually happened. In recording the details of the different Kings in the period of the monarchy it does seem as though we are reading something that looks like reporting. For example, although the following Biblical reference is nothing like a modern newspaper report, it does give the appearance of a straightforward historical claim:

> In the fourteenth year of King Hezekiah, King Sennacherib of Assyria came up against the fortified cities of Judah and captured them (Isaiah 36.1).

To regard the Biblical account of the monarchy as being completely fictitious raises further questions about how the rise of the Israelite state centred in Jerusalem can be explained. There are certainly contradictions in the accounts that are left unresolved and aspects that no historian could know: private and unverifiable elements, including events that occurred behind closed doors; dialogues and even internal monologues. The modern reader has no way of getting back and standing where the original witnesses and participants stood. We have to take much of the story on trust. Most scholars now think that it is very likely that not all the forbears of what became the later twelve tribes of Israel were in Egypt in the time of the liberation from Egypt known as the exodus. But both the Old Testament (Deuteronomy 16.5-9) and the New Testament (1 Corinthians 10.1-4) see that redemptive event as what constituted the life of Israel. If God did not bring Israel out of Egypt, even though the precise historical details may be less clear than a surface reading of the Biblical accounts suggests, then there is no basis for Israel's creeds and its religious celebrations such as the annual festival of the Passover. The faith and theology simply disappears.

A confession of faith

The historicity of the Old Testament is much more complex than either the maximalist or minimalist positions portray, not least because different types of literature assume different ideas of 'truth'. Too often readers overlook the fact that the Bible is not a single book but a whole library made up of many books written in a different 'genre' such as narrative, poetry, prophecy, law, wisdom and apocalyptic. None of these different 'genres' represents the 'truth' in the same way. We must not judge the 'truth' of each of these types of narrative by standards appropriate to the others.

John Goldingay claims that the Bible does not lose its value if it is not wholly factual. He considers, for instance, that the early chapters of Genesis are best regarded as a form of *'imaginative parable'* and are the product of *inspired creativity*. To conclude, as he does, that some of the material in the Garden of Eden story, such as the 'talking snake' and the 'tree of the knowledge of good and evil', are best represented as parable does not mean that the stories are merely fiction and therefore untrue. As Goldingay points out, truth can be conveyed in many forms:

> We must be prepared to reckon that God was involved in the crafting of the story as well as in the events of history, and was involved in crafting the story even when it differed from the history. God likes history, but God also likes stories such as the parables and does not mind mixing them. … God was involved in the events of the biblical story and in the development of a narrative that was sufficiently factual but could incorporate nonfactual material.[5]

As we have seen, recent scholarship has shown that the historical reconstruction of Israel's history – 'what really happened' – is an enterprise fraught with difficulty. This need not deter the person of faith. In many respects, the Scriptures of the Old and New Testaments are not history books, although as Goldingay points out above, they do contain some very good history. But they are quintessentially confessions of faith. Amid all the varying testimonies of the collection of books that

---

5 John Goldingay, *Old Testament Theology*, Volume 1 (IVP, 2003), 878f

make up the canon of the Bible, in a variety of literary styles from different times and places, we are given something like a 2,150-years long account of what God has said and done in human life. And because God is the subject and chief actor in this long, turbulent drama, a solely rationalistic 'historical critical' approach can never fully recover its story. Historical criticism can aid us in the task. It cannot complete it. The faithful reader's task is not to reconstruct Israel's history. Anyone who would deny the veracity of the Old Testament metanarrative is confronted with questions of where this unique covenant people came from and what sustained its life, just as anyone who questions the New Testament's history has to answer the same questions about the church.

Barton and Bowden succinctly sum up the Biblical authors' approach to history when they say:

> The story the Bible tells is not, we believe, based on pure fiction; but the *story* is not *history* in anything like a modern sense of that word. Indeed, what a modern historian can say about each of the periods described here is often very different from what the Old Testament tells us. But without having in our minds the Old Testament's own version of events we cannot understand what the Biblical authors are talking about. We need to empathize with their version before we can grasp what they were trying to say about God, his people and the world.[6]

---

6 John Barton & Julia Bowden, *The Original Story: God, Israel & the World*, (DLT, 2014), 17

Appendix C: Texts of Terror

Those who wish to deride the Christian faith find their sharpest ammunition in the so-called tyrant God of the Old Testament. Richard Dawkins uses a string of adjectives to make his point:

> The God of the Old Testament is arguably the most unpleasant character in all fiction: jealous and proud of it; a petty, unjust, unforgiving control-freak; a vindictive, bloodthirsty ethnic cleanser; a misogynistic, homophobic, racist, infanticidal, genocidal, filiacidal, pestilential, megalomaniacal, sadomasochistic, capriciously malevolent bully.[1]

There can be no disputing that the conquest of the land of Canaan is a grim story of judgment and destruction. At least two traditions exist side by side and it is not easy to see how they fit together. One strand conveys the impression of a swift and successful invasion into Canaanite territory:

> So Joshua took the whole land, according to all that the Lord had spoken to Moses; and Joshua gave it for an inheritance to Israel according to their tribal allotments. And the land had rest from war (Joshua 11.23).

The other strand conveys the impression of a much more drawn out invasion:

> But the people of Judah could not drive out the Jebusites, the inhabitants of Jerusalem; so the Jebusites live with the people of Judah in Jerusalem to this day (Joshua 15.63).

With these unresolved mingled accounts the reader is left with the impression, perhaps deliberately on the author's part, that the period in which the twelve tribes were led by local charismatic judges was one of chaos and lack of cohesion. There are certainly some knotty questions raised about the nature of God in the so-called 'texts of terror'. To some

---

1 Richard Dawkins, *The God Delusion*, (Bantam Press, 2006), 31

extent this objection can be softened a bit by placing the ancient texts in their historical context. Modern interpreters must keep in mind that during the period of the Judges (the period from the death of Joshua to the establishment of the monarchy) there were no International Treaties of Justice. When God made a covenant with Abraham, and promised him the land, it is obvious that others would have to be either ejected or subdued before Abraham's descendants could take possession of it. If the Israelites were ever to get into the promised-land, chaos and warfare were more or less inevitable.

But it is much more important to set the period of warfare under the leadership of the Judges (a period of approximately three hundred years, though there is considerable debate over the exact time frame) in the context of the larger story, which is the story of God's unfolding salvation and universal blessing. God's ultimate plan is to bring peace among all nations and an end to war and all forms of violence. In fact, the Old Testament repeats *ad nauseam* a little creed that speaks of God's character as an expression of love:

> The Lord is gracious and compassionate, slow to anger and abounding in love.

Love is abounding. Punishment is slow. (see Exod. 34.6,7; Num.14.18; Neh. 9.17; Pss 103.8, 17; 145.8; 2 Kings 13.23; 2 Chron 30.9; Jer. 32.18-19; Nah 1.3).

No book of the Old Testament expounds God's unconditional love for his people more exquisitely than the book of the prophet Hosea. Hosea has been called the 'St John of the Old Testament'. No doubt, the prophet had his own domestic experience in mind. Gomer his wife was a prostitute who continued her trade long after the marriage had been entered into, whilst Hosea remained loyal to her. It is his own messy human experience of love that provides Hosea with the inspiration for his theology. Not surprisingly, the Hebrew word used repeatedly for God's love in this oracle is *'chesed'* – 'covenant love'; 'steadfast love'; 'committed love'; a love that keeps on being love. It is a love that goes beyond all human limits.

In chapter 11, the prophet engages with some unforgettable images that evoke the unconditional love of God. As a *father*, God shows 'patient, nurturing love' as he teaches his baby son, Israel (Ephraim) to walk. Small children loved to be picked up when they get tired. God's love was ever there supporting his erring children: *'Yet it was I who taught Ephraim to walk, I took them up in my arms; but they did not know that I healed them'* (11.3). The metaphor then changes from God as a patient nurturing father to that of a mother. So strong is God's love for the covenant people that the prophet likens it to the umbilical cords that connect a mother to her new-born babe. So deeply entwined is God with them: *'I led them with cords of human kindness, with bands of love. I was to them like those who lift infants to their cheeks. I bent down to them and fed them'* (Hos. 11.4). The prophetic spirit searches for new metaphors to bring out the nature of the selfless, stooping love of God.

The prophet goes on to imagine the divine self-talk in a kind of soliloquy, revealing God's own inner feelings. God is depicted in a state of seething conflict, utterly distraught, like an anguished parent who wants to spank the child and hug the child simultaneously. The passage suggests confusion and uncertainty in the mind of God. In an agony of emotional intensity, God cries: *'How can I give you up, Ephraim? How can I hand you over, O Israel? How can I make you like Admah? How can I treat you like Zeboiim? My heart recoils within me; my compassion grows warm and tender. I will not execute my fierce anger; I will not again destroy Ephraim; for I am God and no mortal, the Holy One in your midst, and I will not come in wrath'* (11:8,9). Clearly God's anger here is so severe that the total annihilation of the people is within the compass of God's mind. Yet no sooner has God's righteous indignation commended such an act of punishment than God's love revolts against the prospect and insists that such a course of action is unthinkable. John Dominic Crossan refers to what, at a superficial reading of the text, appears to be 'bipolar characteristics of God'[2].

---

2 John Dominic Crossan, *How To Read The Bible And Still Be A Christian*, (HarperOne, 2015), 238

It must be admitted that Hosea's thoughts of God are very human. He writes of the wounded love of God. God loves and feels and suffers and can be hurt. We have great difficulty in grasping the collision of contradictory emotions of which Hosea speaks.

The resolution of the dilemma comes, as so often with the prophetic literature, at various levels. In the immediate context of Hosea's day, God's paralyzed feelings are resolved by the restoration following the Assyrian conquest – *'I will not come in wrath'* (11:9). Israel, the prophet says, will return to their homeland. But at a more profound level, Christians have seen in this divine dilemma an 'overspill' which points forward to what happened on the cross. The cross is love's self-sacrifice. In the teeth of diabolic machinations, love keeps on being love. Understanding the meaning of love is essential to understanding the Old Testament.

But there is no room for sentimental indulgence in God's love. The Croatian theologian, Miroslav Volf says he once thought that the idea of an angry God was somehow incompatible with the love of God. But then war came to his country. He writes,

> My last resistance to the idea of God's wrath was a casualty of the war in the former Yugoslavia, the region from which I come. According to some estimates, 200,000 people were killed and over 3 million were displaced. My villages and cities were destroyed, my people shelled day in and day out, some of them brutalised beyond imagination, and I could not imagine God not being angry. ... Though I used to complain about the indecency of the idea of God's wrath, I came to think that I would have to rebel against a God who wasn't wrathful at the sight of the world's evil. God isn't wrathful in spite of being love. God is wrathful because God is love.[3]

John Dominic Crossan comes to the same conclusion. He insists that love and justice, like body and soul, cannot be separated:

---

3 Miroslav Volf, *Free of charge: giving and forgiving in a culture stripped of grace*, (Zondervan, 2006), 138, 139

Justice without love may end in brutality, but love without justice
must end in banality. Love empowers justice, and justice embodies
love. Keep both, or get neither.[4]

The question of God's justice needs to be worked out and developed
from within the revelation of God, not outside it. From outside, from
the point of view of the twenty first century sceptic, the books of Joshua
and Judges appear to do little more than recount horrific stories of a
wicked god. Whatever we make of the moral problems presented by
the period of the conquest it represents a relatively short period in the
overall narrative of Old Testament history. It must not be stretched, as
the celebrity New Atheists have done, conveying the impression that
God of the Old Testament is despicably immoral.

4 John Dominic Crossan, *How To Read the Bible & Still Be A Christian*, (HarperOne, 2015), 245

www.ingramcontent.com/pod-product-compliance
Lightning Source LLC
Chambersburg PA
CBHW051425090426
42737CB00014B/2839